DAY BY DAY
Bible

Hendrickson Publishers, Inc.
P.O. Box 3473
Peabody, Massachusetts 01961-3473

ISBN 1 56563 521 3

Original text published in English under the title *Day by Day Bible*
by John Hunt Publishing Ltd, Ropley, Hants, UK.

Designed by Andrew Milne Design
www.milnedesign.co.uk

Printed by South China Printing Co., China

DAY BY DAY
Bible

DAILY DEVOTIONS FOR
READING WITH CHILDREN

with Bible Time • Talk Time • Prayer Time

Written & illustrated by Eira Reeves

HENDRICKSON
PUBLISHERS

THE BIBLE

What is the Bible?

The Bible is God's special book and it's His way of speaking to us as it teaches about Him and Jesus, His son, and the Holy Spirit.

When did the Bible begin?

It is believed that Moses wrote the first five books of the Old Testament: Genesis, Exodus, Leviticus, Numbers, and Deuteronomy. God also spoke to Moses on a mountain and God's finger wrote on two stones giving ten rules called the Ten Commandments. Since then the stories in the Bible covered thousands and thousands of years.

Who else wrote the Bible?

Besides Moses, God spoke to many different men, and they wrote down all that they had seen and heard from God. Some writers wrote of what was happening around them.

Some books told of God's rules for our lives, while some of the books contained beautiful poetry, wisdom, and songs. Others wrote about events to come.

What was the Bible first written on?

The first words of the Bible were written on clay. Then, many years later, people discovered that they could make paper. So the words of the Bible were put on a scroll of paper and rolled up. This way the Bible could be easily carried around. All the Old Testament was made like this.

Much later the Bible was put into book form. It may have been the first Christians who did this, as they wanted to safely protect all the words that God had given them.

How many books are there in the Bible?

All together there are sixty-six books in the Bible.

In the Old Testament there are 39 books:

Genesis, Exodus, Leviticus, Numbers, Deuteronomy, Joshua, Judges, Ruth, 1 Samuel, 2 Samuel, 1 Kings, 2 Kings, 1 Chronicles, 2 Chronicles, Ezra, Nehemiah, Esther, Job, Psalms, Proverbs, Ecclesiastes, Song of Songs, Isaiah, Jeremiah, Lamentations, Ezekiel, Daniel, Hosea, Joel, Amos, Obadiah, Jonah, Micah, Nahum, Habakkuk, Zephaniah, Haggai, Zechariah, Malachi.

In the New Testament there are 27 books:

Matthew, Mark, Luke, John, Acts, Romans, 1 Corinthians, 2 Corinthians, Galatians, Ephesians, Philippians, Colossians, 1 Thessalonians, 2 Thessalonians, 1 Timothy, 2 Timothy, Titus, Philemon, Hebrews, James, 1 Peter, 2 Peter, 1 John, 2 John, 3 John, Jude, Revelation.

What are the gospels?

These are four books in the beginning of the New Testament. God's Holy Spirit helped four men who followed Jesus to write about His life. "Gospel" means "good news."

How can we learn from the Bible?

God gives us the Holy Spirit to understand His words in the Bible so that we can learn and obey what He says. It also gives us great happiness and joy to know that God can speak to us from His words in the Bible.

The Bible teaches us right from wrong as it is a book of truth. God's words will never change and will last forever and ever!

Have fun in the following pages learning about God's word and stories from the Bible...

OLD TESTAMENT

Contents

	Page		Page
In the beginning	8-13	David's friend Jonathan	111
Adam and Eve	14-19	David and King Saul	112-113
Noah	20-27	King David	114-123
Abram and Sarai	28-31	King Solomon	124-131
Abraham and Sarah	32-35	Elijah, the prophet	132-136
Isaac	36	False prophets	137-141
Esau and Jacob	37-38	Elijah and Elisha	142
Jacob	39-41	Kings of Israel	143-144
Jacob's family	42-45	Elijah leaves	145-146
Joseph	46-47	Elisha	147-150
Joseph in Egypt	48-52	Naaman	151-155
Moses	53-56	Jeremiah	156-157
God talks to Moses	57-58	Daniel	158-161
Moses and Pharaoh	59-61	King Nebuchadnezzar	162-165
Escape from Egypt	62-69	A golden statue	166-167
Joshua	70-79	A fire	168-169
Gideon	80-85	Daniel prays	170-172
Samuel	86-92	Daniel in the den	173-174
Saul	93-98	Rebuilding Jerusalem	175-181
David the shepherd	99-104	Prophets	182-191
David and Goliath	105-110		

The Old Testament
Introduction

The Bible starts right at the beginning.
In the beginning was God. He saw
that He could make a beautiful world
out of the darkness.
He created everything in the world...sky, water,
plants, flowers, trees, animals, and fishes

... and then people.

Then things began to go wrong in the world.
But God had a plan to save His people.

The Old Testament is about God's
plan unfolding and God showing His people,
the Israelites, His land,
and all the events that took place
in this nation.

He promised them
one day, to send someone
to take care of them and save them.

His name is Jesus.

BIBLE TIME
Genesis 1: verses 1-3

Only darkness

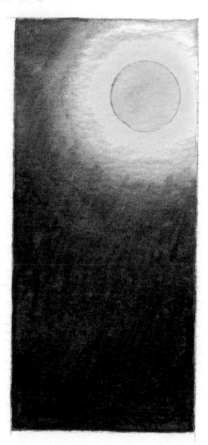

Many, many years ago there was only darkness. There was absolutely nothing! But God saw that out of the darkness He could make something really beautiful and wonderful. So God said to the darkness, "Let there be light!" and light appeared.

It was so bright and brilliant – God was delighted!

The light shone brightly through all of the darkness.

TALK TIME
If you switch on a light what happens?

PRAYER TIME
Dear God, I am so happy that you brought light into the world and turned it from darkness. Help me to enjoy the day time when it's light. Amen

BIBLE TIME
Genesis 1: verses 6-10

Water and sky and land

Next God wanted to see water and so He made lots and lots of it! Then He spoke again and made the air above it into sky... blue, blue sky. So far everything was looking wonderful to God. He was so very pleased.

He then wanted to add to the water and sky so He made some dry ground that He called "land." It divided the water which He called "sea". God was even more delighted with what He had made!

TALK TIME
How can water be used?

PRAYER TIME
Dear God, I think you are so clever to have made the whole world. I enjoy looking at your sky and water. Thank you for water for drinking, for watering the earth so that plants can grow, and for me to bathe in! Amen.

BIBLE TIME
Genesis 1: verses 11-13

Lots of trees and flowers

Now God created plants and trees that started to grow. There were small bushy plants, big trees, and vegetables and flowers that were all different sizes and beautiful colors.

The trees had different shapes of leaves and some had fruit that looked delicious.

Everything was a mass of wonderful colors.

God looked at it all and was so very pleased with what He had done so far.

TALK TIME
If you had a garden, what would you like to grow in it?

PRAYER TIME
Dear God, thank you that you have given us all the different plants and colorful flowers for us to enjoy and to look at. Thank you for fresh vegetables and fruit for us to eat every day. Amen.

BIBLE TIME
Genesis 1: verses 14-19

Different times

Now God wanted different times for
His world, so He put a sun in the sky that
would shine in the day and give light, and
He made a moon and hundreds and
hundreds of stars that would shine at night.

The world now had a daytime and a night time.

God also made times and seasons of the year. These
were called Spring, Summer, Autumn, and Winter.

God was even more pleased
with what He had done.

He saw that everything
was good!

TALK TIME
What is your favorite season?
Why?

PRAYER TIME
Dear God, you make all different things for us to enjoy.
Spring flowers, summer warmth from the sun, autumn leaves
falling, and snow in the winter. Thank you. Amen.

BIBLE TIME
Genesis 1: verses 20-23

Birds and fishes

   Now God wanted more in His beautiful world. So He created birds and fish. All sorts!

Some birds flew high in the sky, some birds had big wings, some had small wings. All of them had different colored feathers!

Then God filled the waters with fish. They swam and jumped and chased each other from the bottom of the sea to the top. God was even more pleased with what He saw!

TALK TIME

Which birds do you like? Try to name some of the birds in the pictures.

PRAYER TIME

Dear God, you are so marvelous, creating all the fishes that swim in the water and all the birds that fly in the sky. Thank you. Amen.

BIBLE TIME
Genesis 1: verses 24-25

Loads of animals

"Let's have more!" God said. "Let there be creatures and wild animals!"

Wow! All sorts of animals appeared... all sorts of colors and sizes, some with long necks, some had smooth hair and some had prickles, some ate grass and some ate leaves.

God smiled at everything He had made in the world so far.

TALK TIME
Do you have a pet? Do you know of a friend who has a pet? What kind of animal is it and what is its name?

PRAYER TIME
Dear God, you are so clever when you speak and then create all the animals that are so very different. Thank you that we can enjoy them. Amen.

BIBLE TIME
Genesis 1: verses 26-31
Genesis 2: verse 22

God's friends

Then God did something extraordinary!

After all that He had created, God desired something very special. He wanted to have friends that He could walk with and talk to. So out of the dust of the earth He made a man and then He made a woman. He named them Adam and Eve. God wanted His two friends to enjoy the lovely garden He had made for them.

God also wanted them to be His friends.

TALK TIME
God really wanted friends to love. Are you God's friend?

PRAYER TIME
Dear God, thank you for making such a beautiful garden for Adam and Eve to enjoy. Thank you for gardens that I can enjoy! Amen.

BIBLE TIME
Genesis 2: verses 2-3

A day of rest

God had created everything on the earth, and it was beautiful. He was so very pleased with it. Then God took a day of rest.

God wanted this day of rest to be holy, a day apart from other days. He wanted it to be an important day for worshipping Him and all that He had created.

God blessed this day of rest for it was a day that belonged to Him.

TALK TIME

What do you like to do when you rest? Which day is important to you for just being with your family, enjoying one another, and relaxing together?

PRAYER TIME

Dear God, thank you for a day of rest so we can worship you. Thank you for blessing this day. Amen.

BIBLE TIME
Genesis 2: verses 15-18

Not for you!

Adam and Eve so enjoyed walking and talking in the garden with God. They loved all the special world that He had made for them. It was perfect and beautiful!

Now God pointed to one tree in the middle of the garden and said to them, "Don't touch!" and then He said, "The fruit on that tree is not good for you."

God wanted to trust His two friends and He didn't want them to come to any harm in His garden He had created for them.

TALK TIME
If someone said to you, "Don't touch" something, what would you do?

PRAYER TIME
Dear God, I am so glad you give us rules to live by. Help me to obey them. Amen.

BIBLE TIME
Genesis 3: verses 1-6

A snake appears

One day a serpent slithered by. He was craftier than any of the other animals. He looked at Adam and Eve and asked a question,

"Has God told you not to eat fruit from one tree?"

Eve pointed to the tree that God had spoken about.

"Oh, don't be so stupid!" said the serpent, "It's perfectly all right to eat from it. Try a fruit."

Eve didn't think it would cause any harm, and so she took a fruit and bit into it. Then she offered it to Adam.

In that one moment they had chosen to disobey God.

TALK TIME
Have you seen anyone recently who has been naughty?
What did they do?

PRAYER TIME
Dear God, please help me to always obey you and try not to be naughty. Amen.

BIBLE TIME
Genesis 3: verses 8-13, 23-24

I blame you!

In the stillness of the evening God called Adam and Eve by their names... but they didn't answer. When God found them, they were trying to hide from Him. God asked Adam if they had eaten a fruit from the tree. Adam blamed Eve for picking the fruit. God then asked Eve about it, and she blamed the serpent.

God was very sad.

From that day onward God couldn't allow them in His beautiful garden. Adam and Eve had spoiled everything that God had made for them.

TALK TIME

How do you think God felt when Adam and Eve had done what He had told them not to do?
When you have done something wrong, what do you do?

PRAYER TIME

Dear God, I am sorry that Adam and Eve were naughty.
I am sorry if sometimes I am naughty, too. Please forgive me.
Amen.

BIBLE TIME
Genesis 3: verses 17-19

A troubled world

Trouble had come into the world now... all because Adam and Eve had disobeyed God.

They walked sadly out of the beautiful garden, and God knew from that moment on life would be difficult for Adam and Eve. They had changed His world forever.

Never again would they be part of God's garden and all the beautiful things He had created for them.

They had to leave everything.

TALK TIME
How do you think Adam and Eve felt after making God sad? How does it make you feel?

PRAYER TIME
Dear God, I am so sorry that Adam and Eve spoiled your world. I know that you created the world for us to enjoy. Please help me to see all the beautiful things you have made for me. Amen.

BIBLE TIME
Genesis 6: verses 5-8

Bad people

Slowly the number of people increased on God's earth.

But they also fought and quarreled among themselves.
They hurt one another and spoiled God's world. They didn't even love God.

God was very unhappy with the wickedness of man.

He wanted to make His world into a much better place and change it, but He needed the help of a very special and kind person. That's when He saw Noah. Noah was different from all the other people.

Noah loved God.

TALK TIME
Are there are people around you who squabble and argue? How do you think you could help them?

PRAYER TIME
Dear God, I want to love you as Noah did, so that other people around me who are unkind can see how much I love you. Amen.

BIBLE TIME
Genesis 6: verses 13-16

A boat SO large

Noah heard God tell him to build
a boat – a really BIG one.
So Noah started to draw up plans. His neighbors asked,
"What is it for?" "Are you sure you heard God speak to you?"
"Why do you need such a great, BIG boat?" and they laughed at Noah.

Noah ignored them. He was sure of what he had heard God say. God was going to destroy the earth because people had become so wicked.

But God also said that He would save Noah and his family.

TALK TIME
When a parent, caregiver, or teacher tells you to do something, do you find it easy or hard to obey?

PRAYER TIME
Dear God, I want to do what I am told. Please help me to be good. Amen.

BIBLE TIME
Genesis 6: verses 17-18

God's plan

So Noah started to work on building the boat. He looked at the plan that God had given him and then started to saw up wood, and pound nails in... bang, bang, bang. He was busy all day long. Neighbors watched and watched him and wondered what he was doing. Why was he building such a huge boat?

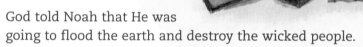

God told Noah that He was going to flood the earth and destroy the wicked people.

So Noah worked and worked hard building the boat that God told him to build.

TALK TIME
Have you ever built anything? Did you enjoy building it? Describe what you made.

PRAYER TIME
Dear God, I think it is great how Noah listened to you and your plans. Help me to hear what you want me to do. Amen.

BIBLE TIME
Genesis 6: verses 18-21

Two of every animal

Then God told Noah to gather up his family and also to collect two of all the animals, birds, and creatures. What a job! But Noah obeyed, and slowly two of every kind of animal went on board. Imagine that... a boat full of animals and no water anywhere!

Noah then took all types of food onto the boat to feed the animals.

A while later a few raindrops began to fall. God told Noah to take his family inside the boat. God closed the door.

TALK TIME

If you had been there with Noah, what would you have thought as you saw all the animals go into the boat... and no water around?

PRAYER TIME

Dear God, thank you that you know everything that will happen and that you knew all along why you told Noah to build the boat. Amen.

BIBLE TIME
Genesis 7: verses 17-19

It begins to rain

After Noah, his family, all the animals and birds and creatures, and all the food went onto the boat, it began to rain... and rain... and rain.

It rained for forty nights and forty days and the boat floated and floated. The winds howled and howled and the rain fell and splashed on the boat as it floated higher and higher above the ground.

Gradually the water rose until it reached the tops of the mountains.

But Noah, his family, and all the animals, birds, and creatures were safe inside the boat, just as God had said.

TALK TIME

Do you like the rain? When it's really windy and raining hard, would you like to be indoors or outdoors. Why?

PRAYER TIME

Dear God, thank you that you kept Noah safe in the storm. I know that when it is stormy, you will keep me safe, too. Amen.

BIBLE TIME
Genesis 8: verses 3-14

Dry land

After a very, very long time the boat floated and then got stuck on top of a mountain.

Noah looked out of the window.

To check that it had really stopped raining, Noah sent out a dove. It returned the first time, because it couldn't find a tree to perch on. So a bit later Noah sent the dove out again, and this time the dove returned with a green olive branch in its beak.

"Hooray!" said Noah, "the water has gone down."

Then Noah sent out the dove again and this time it didn't return.

Noah knew it was safe now to come out of the boat. He knew that God had protected him, his family, and all the animals, birds, and creatures during the storm.

TALK TIME
Does this story make you want to trust God?
What are some ways you can trust God at home or at school?

PRAYER TIME
Dear God, I am so grateful that I can always trust you because you protected Noah in the flood. Amen.

Hooray, no rain

God was pleased that Noah had done all that He had asked him and said, "Come out of the boat with all of your family and all of the animals and birds and fill the earth again with children."

Noah opened the door and led all the animals, birds, and creatures from the boat. They ran and jumped for joy at being on dry ground again!

God promised Noah that He would never again destroy living creatures on the earth. Noah was very happy.

TALK TIME
What is your favorite animal and why?

PRAYER TIME
Dear God, thank you that you saved Noah, all of his family, and all of the animals, birds, and creatures, because now I can enjoy them. Amen.

BIBLE TIME
Genesis 9: verses 1-17

A rainbow

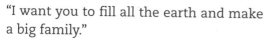

When Noah and all
the animals were
out of the boat,
God said to Noah,
"I want you to fill all the earth and make
a big family."

To show Noah that He would always keep His
promise never to flood the earth again, God
painted a big rainbow in the sky. It was
beautiful and it stretched right over
the earth, showing that it was a
fresh new beginning for Noah and
his family.

God wanted to bless them.

TALK TIME
What do like about a rainbow?
Can you say the colors of the rainbow?
Have you ever made a promise to someone? Did you keep it?

PRAYER TIME
Dear God, show us ways to take care of the animals in the world.
Thank you for your lovely rainbow in the sky. Help me to always try
to keep a promise that I make to someone. Amen.

ABRAM AND SARAI Day 21

BIBLE TIME
Genesis 12: verses 1-5

Go

A man named Abram and his wife named Sarai lived in Haran. They didn't have any children and they were very sad about this.

Abram was a very rich man. He had lots of sheep and camels and goats and was very wealthy. One day God spoke to him and said, "I want you to leave Haran and go to another country I will show you. I will also give you a big family, and I will bless you."

Abram didn't question God because he trusted Him. So with his wife, family, servants, and his nephew Lot and his family, he packed up all his belongings and set off to find this new land that God would show him. What an adventure!

Abram trusted God.

TALK TIME
Have you ever had an adventure when you have had to trust God? When?

PRAYER TIME
Dear God, I thank you that you are my heavenly Father. I trust that you will always walk with me, and I will know that you are by my side wherever I go. Amen.

BIBLE TIME
Genesis 13: verses 5-11

A new land

Eventually Abram came to the land that God had promised him. It was called Canaan. Abram and Lot had hundreds and hundreds of animals in their care.

The land of Canaan was very green and had plenty of grass for the herds to eat. It also had many flowing streams of water for them to drink from.

But the land could not support all of the animals Abram and Lot had. So an argument started between their servants about which piece of land they would take.

"Don't let's quarrel," Abram said to Lot. "You choose the piece of land you want."

So Lot chose the best piece of land. It had the most water and plenty of green grass.

TALK TIME
Have you ever been in a quarrel? Why did it start and how did it end?

PRAYER TIME
Dear God, please don't let me get involved in quarrels and help me never to grab the best for myself among my friends. Help me to be like Abram. Amen.

BIBLE TIME

Genesis 13: verse 13
Genesis 14: verses 12-16

Enemies

Now the land that Lot had chosen was indeed very rich with plenty for the animals to eat and drink. But the people on this piece of land were very wicked. They had lots of enemies and were always fighting them.

They even took Lot and his family as prisoners. Poor Lot! In the beginning he thought he had chosen the best piece of land but now it turned out to be the worst choice.

When Abram heard about Lot's trouble, he went to his rescue. He immediately saved Lot and his servants from their enemies.

TALK TIME

Have any of your friends been through difficult times? Can you talk about it? What are some ways you can help your friends through these times?

PRAYER TIME

Dear heavenly Father, help me to have a heart like Abram and let other people choose first and go to the rescue of friends when they are having a bad time. Amen.

BIBLE TIME
Genesis 15: verses 4-5

You're not too old

Abram and Sarai his wife were very sad. Although they were rich they didn't have any children. They were very, very old – too old to have children, they thought, but Abram trusted God for everything and so he prayed.

That night God asked Abram to come out of his tent, and He said to him,

"Look up at the stars. See if you can count them all. There will be more people in your family than all the stars in the sky!"

God meant that Abram would be a father and grandfather to many, many, many children!

TALK TIME
Do you have a grandmother or grandfather or an older friend of the family? Ask them about happy memories that they have of people and times in their lives.

PRAYER TIME
Dear God, thank you that you spoke to Abram so, so long ago and gave him a promise. Thank you for people that I know like grandpas and grandmas and older friends. Please take care of them. Amen.

31

BIBLE TIME
Genesis 17: verses 5-7 and 15-18

Change of name

Abram was now 99 and Sarai his wife was 90. God had promised them children. But because of this promise God wanted to change their names. He gave Abram the name of Abraham, which means "father of many" and he changed Sarai's name to "Sarah", which means "princess."

God said that he would bless Sarah so that she would become the mother of a special son. They were to call him Isaac, which means "he laughs."

Abraham had difficulty in believing what God had told them. Surely they were both far too old to have children!

But he laughed and chuckled at the thought of it!

TALK TIME
Do you know the meaning of your name? Go to a library and get a book that gives the meaning of names.

PRAYER TIME
Dear heavenly Father, thank you that you know each one of us by our name. Thank you that we are so special to you. Amen.

BIBLE TIME
Genesis 18: verses 1-10

Visitors

Abraham was sitting at the entrance to his tent. In the distance Abraham saw three people coming toward his tent. He thought they were just travelers in the desert. He immediately shouted to Sarah to bring out the best food for them.

The visitors were no ordinary visitors, though. They were angels in disguise and had brought a message from God!

One of the visitors said to Abraham, "In a year's time you and your wife will have a son."

TALK TIME
When was the last time you had visitors at your house?
What did you and your family do to make them feel special?

PRAYER TIME
Dear heavenly Father, please help visitors feel welcome in our house, and if I am a visitor in someone else's home, help me to be good, friendly, and polite. Amen.

Sarah laughs

Now Sarah was inside the tent when the visitors were enjoying their meal. She was also eavesdropping, which meant she hid and overheard their conversation.

Did she hear right? They were going to have a baby in a year's time? Surely not!

She began to laugh and laugh and giggle and giggle. How could she believe the conversation she had just overheard from inside the tent? She didn't believe that Abraham and she could have a baby. They were far too old!

TALK TIME
Have you ever read or heard anything about God that you found hard to believe? Talk about it.

PRAYER TIME
Dear God, help me to always believe what you say in the Bible so that my faith in you will become stronger and stronger. Amen.

BIBLE TIME
Genesis 21: verses 1-7

A new baby

As God promised, Sarah became pregnant.

Abraham was 100 years old. That's very, very old to become a dad!

The baby arrived just as God said it would. Can you imagine how Abraham and Sarah felt? God's promise had seemed so outrageous, and yet now it had all come true... here was the baby they had been promised. Abraham and Sarah gave him the name of Isaac just as God had asked. Now they laughed again, for they knew that baby Isaac had been given to them by God.

TALK TIME
Do you know of a mother who has just had a baby?
What did she name the baby?

PRAYER TIME
Dear God, thank you for all the joy and laughter you bring into our lives. Thank you for all moms and newly born babies everywhere. Amen.

ISAAC Day 29

BIBLE TIME
**Genesis 24: verses 1-4
and verses 61-67**

A wedding

When Isaac grew up to be a young man, Abraham wanted a good wife for him. Abraham knew God would help him. So he sent his servant out to bring back a wife for Isaac.

The servant went on a long journey to find a young woman. Eventually he found Rebekah and returned home with her. Abraham was pleased when he saw Rebekah. When Isaac met her, he knew that she would make a lovely wife. They were soon married.

It was a wonderful wedding celebration! Abraham was so happy that Isaac had married.

TALK TIME
What was your favorite party? Can you remember what you did and the food you ate and who was at the party?

PRAYER TIME
Dear heavenly Father, thank you for all the things we celebrate. Thank you for the parties I enjoy and being with all my friends. Amen.

BIBLE TIME
Genesis 27: verses 5-30

JACOB   ESAU

Two sons

Later on, Isaac and Rebekah had twin sons. One was named Esau and the other was named Jacob. Esau had red hair and grew up to be strong and enjoyed hunting animals. Jacob was quiet and loved to stay at home.

When Isaac became old and blind, he wanted to give the family blessing to his favorite son Esau. He asked Esau to bring him his favorite food.

However, Jacob wanted the family blessing. So his mother dressed him up to look like Esau to trick his father.

"Here you are, Father," said Jacob, pretending to be Esau, "I have cooked you some delicious food." Isaac, the father, thought it was his favorite son and he blessed Jacob and not Esau. Jacob had tricked Isaac!

TALK TIME
Have you ever known anyone who tricked someone?
Explain what happened.

PRAYER TIME
Dear God, please help me to understand that it is not nice to fool someone. Help me to be always truthful and not like Jacob. Amen.

BIBLE TIME
Genesis 27: verses 30-43

Jacob cheats Esau

A little later on, after Jacob had tricked Isaac, Esau returned home, bringing food for his blind father.

"I'm home," he said cheerfully. "I have a meal for you, Father, and I look forward to getting the family blessing from you."

"But, Esau, I have already given you the blessing!" said Isaac.

Esau stopped in front of his blind father.

He knew immediately that his brother Jacob had tricked him and had taken the family blessing instead.

He was so angry that he wanted to kill his brother.

TALK TIME
What are your thoughts on Jacob cheating his brother?
Have you ever seen or heard of anyone cheating?

PRAYER TIME
Dear heavenly Father, I am sorry that Jacob cheated his brother. I know this must have made you sad. Help me to understand how cheating hurts other people. Amen.

BIBLE TIME

Genesis 27: verses 42-45;
Genesis 28: verses 1-2

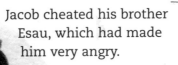

Runaway Jacob

Jacob cheated his brother Esau, which had made him very angry.

Rebekah, their mother, called for Jacob.

"Listen," she said to him. "You must leave immediately. Your brother knows that you cheated him and wants to kill you. You must run away now!"

Jacob hurriedly got his belongings together. His father Isaac came to say goodbye to him. Although he knew that Jacob had lied to him he loved his son and was so sorry to see him leave home. "May God bless you," Isaac, the father, said to Jacob. "Go to your Uncle Laban's home and live there."

TALK TIME

Have you ever had to say goodbye to someone who has moved away? Can you say how you felt?

PRAYER TIME

Dear God, help me when I feel sad when I have to say goodbye to someone I love. Amen.

BIBLE TIME
Genesis 28: verses 10-12

A dream!

Jacob ran and ran and ran! It got
very late, and it was dark. Jacob was
tired from running.

He found a place to rest far from anywhere.

He put a stone for a pillow and wrapped himself up
and fell into a deep sleep.

But something very special happened. As Jacob slept, he began to
dream. In his dream he saw angels coming down and going up a
ladder to Heaven.

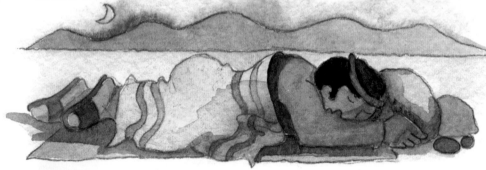

TALK TIME

Can you remember a dream that you have had?
What was it about?

PRAYER TIME

Dear heavenly Father, it is good to have nice dreams, and
I thank you for those. But please help me when I have had a
bad dream, and let me know that you are close. Amen.

BIBLE TIME
Genesis 28: verses 13-15

God takes care

When Jacob saw angels on the ladder in his dream, he looked at the top of the ladder and saw God. God spoke to him and said, "I am going to give you a BIG, BIG family, and many people will be blessed through your family."

God continued to speak to him, "I will always be with you and watch over you wherever you go. I will never leave you."

Jacob knew he had met God in his dream and that God had spoken to him.

TALK TIME
How does God speak to you? When was the last time you knew that God had spoken to you? What did you think He said?

PRAYER TIME
Dear God, thank you that you spoke to Jacob in a dream. Thank you, too, that you said you would never leave Jacob. Thank you that I know that you will never leave me. Amen.

BIBLE TIME
Genesis 29: verses 16-30

Jacob marries

After running a long distance from Esau, Jacob arrived at Laban's home and was welcomed. Laban had two daughters, and Jacob wanted to marry one of them. Her name was Rachel. Jacob said to Laban that, instead of money, he would work for free for seven years so that Rachel could be his wife.

But such a sad thing happened to Jacob after seven years... on the wedding day Laban sent his older daughter Leah to marry him.

Laban had tricked Jacob!

So Jacob had to work another seven years so that he could marry Rachel, whom he really loved.

TALK TIME
What do you think of Laban doing this to Jacob? Has anyone ever played a trick on you? What did you do about it?

PRAYER TIME
Dear Father God, you know that it isn't very nice for people to play tricks on one another. Please would you teach us how to be loving to one another. Amen.

BIBLE TIME
Genesis 30: verses 1-24

A BIG, BIG *family*

Jacob lived with Laban and his family for a long time. After many years Jacob's own family began to grow in a big way. Altogether he had twelve sons and one daughter!

These are the names that Jacob gave them... Reuben, Simeon, Levi, Judah, Issachar, Zebulun, Benjamin, Dan, Naphtali, Gad, Asher, and Joseph, and the daughter was named Dinah.

This was just as God had told Jacob in his dream many years before: he would have a big family!

Out of all his sons, Jacob had a favorite one, and that was Joseph.

TALK TIME
How big is your family? Can you say all of their names?

PRAYER TIME
Dear God, I love the way that you keep your promises. Help me to believe in the promises you give to me. Amen

BIBLE TIME
Genesis 32: verses 3-6

Messengers

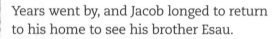

Years went by, and Jacob longed to return to his home to see his brother Esau.

But the last time Jacob had seen Esau he had tricked him.

Jacob decided to send a messenger to Esau. He said to the messenger, "Go to my brother Esau and ask him if he will forgive me. Tell him that I have stayed at Uncle Laban's home, and I will send him gifts."

Jacob told his servants to go ahead of him with all the gifts for Esau.

Then Jacob got all his family and animals together and started the long journey back to his home.

He was looking forward to seeing Esau, but he wondered how his brother would greet him.

TALK TIME

When you have been away from your home, what do you miss? How do you feel going back home?

PRAYER TIME

Dear God, Thank you for our homes that you have given us. Thank you that you are always with us when we are away from our home and when we are in our home. Amen.

JACOB'S FAMILY Day 38

BIBLE TIME
Genesis 33: verses 4-11

A great greeting

After walking many miles with his family and animals, Jacob saw a person in the distance.

It was his brother Esau.

What joy! Esau was so happy to see Jacob that he ran towards him with his arms held out wide to give him a hug. They even cried together with happiness! Esau loved all the gifts Jacob had sent to him, and he had forgiven his brother for the trick he had played on him.

There was so much joy in the family!

TALK TIME

Has there ever been an argument between your brothers or sisters or in your family? What happened?

PRAYER TIME

Dear heavenly Father, Thank you that you put us in families. Thank you for your love for my mom/dad/brother/sister/caregivers. Help us not to argue and, if we do, help us to go to one another and say sorry. Amen.

BIBLE TIME
Genesis 37: verses 3-8

What a coat

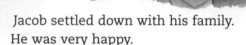

Jacob settled down with his family. He was very happy.

Now Jacob really loved his youngest son Joseph, so he made him the most beautiful and colorful coat. When Joseph put it on, he showed off in front of his brothers. They all became so jealous of him because they saw that their father Jacob loved Joseph more than them.

One night Joseph had a dream and told his brothers. The dream meant that all his brothers would bow down to him.

His brothers hated him even more!

TALK TIME
What would you have said to Joseph and why?

PRAYER TIME
Dear God, thank you that you love us all the same. Help us not to show off like Joseph. Amen.

BIBLE TIME
Genesis 37: verses 28-36

Get rid of him

Joseph had upset his brothers so much that they decided to get rid of him. So they sold him to some passing travelers who were going to Egypt. They didn't tell Jacob, their father, what they had done.

A little while later they told Jacob that they had found Joseph's beautiful coat... but not Joseph.

"My son must be lost!" Jacob said. He cried for days because his favorite son had disappeared. Meanwhile Joseph was on his way to Egypt.

TALK TIME
What do you think God must have thought when He saw the brothers sell their brother, Joseph?

PRAYER TIME
Dear heavenly Father, thank you that you knew the wonderful plan for Joseph. Thank you that you kept him safe. Amen.

BIBLE TIME
Genesis 39: verses 1-6

Joseph is sold

Joseph and the travelers arrived in Egypt after a very long journey. When they arrived, they sold Joseph to one of Pharaoh's captains, who put Joseph to work in his house.

Now God was with Joseph, and everything he did for the captain was good. So the captain put him in charge of his whole house.

Joseph worked well and the captain trusted him.

The captain knew that God was with Joseph for he saw Him bless the whole household.

TALK TIME
What happens when God blesses you or someone you know?

PRAYER TIME
Dear God, I get so excited when I see you bless other friends. I want to thank you when this happens. Amen.

BIBLE TIME
Genesis 41: verses 33-41

Plenty of food

Joseph had lots of
adventures in Egypt.
He was very much liked
by Pharaoh.

Pharaoh put him in
charge of all the land,
and over time Joseph
stored a lot of grain in the
storehouses.

There was so much in the
storehouses for the people in
Egypt to eat.

Pharaoh was so pleased with Joseph that he
put him in charge of his whole palace. Pharaoh said,
"I can't find a man as good as Joseph in all of my land. I've put him
in charge and given him the top job."

TALK TIME
Do you know people in charge? Can you name some of them?

PRAYER TIME
*Dear God, thank you for all the people in charge. May you give
them wisdom when they lead us. Amen.*

BIBLE TIME

*Genesis 41: verse 54
and Genesis 42: verses 1-10*

Seeking food

Now in the country where Joseph's father Jacob lived, there was no food to eat... there was a famine. So Jacob said to all of his sons, "We have no food here. You must all go to Egypt, for they have lots of food to eat."

So they all set out to go to Egypt. After miles and miles of walking they arrived in Egypt, to the place where Joseph was in charge, but they didn't recognize him.

But Joseph recognized his brothers and gave orders to fill their bags with grain.

His brothers were so glad to get food!

TALK TIME

Famine means no food for people to eat. Do you know of any countries today that are very poor and have no food? How can you help them?

PRAYER TIME

Dear heavenly Father, please will you show me ways to help other people who have no food. Amen.

BIBLE TIME
Genesis 45: verses 4-15

I'm your brother

When Joseph's brothers had bought the grain from him, Joseph very gently said to them, "I am your long lost brother, and I have forgiven you for selling me to those travelers all those years ago. I know that God has been with me all this time in Egypt."

The brothers were so delighted meeting Joseph again! They couldn't believe it. They threw their arms round him. They were amazed how well Joseph had done in Egypt.

Joseph knew that meeting his family again was all part of God's plan for him.

TALK TIME
Who would you like to meet that you haven't seen for a long time? Why?

PRAYER TIME
Dear God, thank you that you knew what would happen to Joseph. Thank you that you brought all the family together and that they were happy. Amen.

BIBLE TIME
Genesis 47: verses 7-12

Blessings

Now Jacob, the father, had joined all of his sons in Egypt. He was so very happy to see Joseph again! Pharaoh asked Joseph what his brothers did for jobs.

"They are all shepherds," Joseph told him.

Then Pharaoh said to Joseph that his father and all his brothers were welcome to settle and work in Egypt.

How great that Joseph could now supply them with food and houses!

All the family were so pleased that they were all together again in Egypt.

TALK TIME
When your family gets together, what do you like to do?

PRAYER TIME
Dear heavenly Father, thank you that you brought Joseph's family together. Thank you that you love to see happiness in families. Please be with us as a family. Amen.

BIBLE TIME
Exodus 1: verses 7-14

Slaves

After many, many years of staying in Egypt, God's people, called the Hebrews, had grown to be a BIG, BIG family. And they all worked very hard.

Now there was a different Pharaoh, and he did not like to see so many Hebrews in his country. So he decided to make them slaves, forcing them to make bricks and working in the fields. He had Egyptian slave masters standing over them and giving harsh orders.

The slave masters were very cruel to the Hebrews and made them work even harder.

TALK TIME
What would you have said to the Pharaoh?

PRAYER TIME
Dear God, it is a comfort to know that even when people go through very sad times you are with them.
Thank you that you are with me when I feel sad. Amen.

BIBLE TIME
Exodus 1: verses 15 –16;
Exodus 2: verses 1-4

A horrible order

Pharaoh became scared that there were too
many Hebrews in the land of Egypt and gave an order that every
Hebrew baby boy was to be killed.

On hearing this command one Hebrew mother wanted to hide her
beautiful baby from Pharaoh. She didn't want him to die. So she
carefully put the baby into a basket and placed him among the
bulrushes in the river.

The baby's sister stood by, watching to see that he was safe.

TALK TIME
Talk about something that makes you sad.

PRAYER TIME
*Dear heavenly Father, thank you that you gave wisdom to this
baby's mother. Thank you that you kept this baby safe. Amen.*

BIBLE TIME
Exodus 2: verses 5-10

A baby found

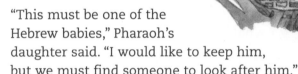

Pharaoh's daughter decided to take a walk along the river with her friends. As they walked they saw the basket among the bulrushes. They looked inside and to their surprise they found a baby.

"This must be one of the Hebrew babies," Pharaoh's daughter said. "I would like to keep him, but we must find someone to look after him."

The sister went and found the baby's mother, and Pharaoh's daughter asked her to take care of the baby at the Royal Palace.

Pharaoh's daughter named the baby Moses.

TALK TIME
Moses means "drawn from the water". How special is it to you that God knows you by your name?

PRAYER TIME
Dear God, thank you that you know each one of us by name. Thank you that Moses was very special to you. Thank you that I, too, am very special to you. Amen.

BIBLE TIME
Exodus 2: verses 11-23

Growing up

Moses was brought up as a Royal Prince in Pharaoh's Egyptian Palace even though he was a Hebrew. One day Moses went out into the fields and saw an Egyptian beating a Hebrew man. Moses killed the Egyptian and hid him in the sand.

When Pharaoh heard about it, he was furious and wanted to kill Moses for what he had done to one of his men.

Moses was frightened and ran away; he hid in a place called Midian.

At the same time in Egypt all the Hebrews were crying out to God to rescue them from being slaves.

TALK TIME
Have you ever cried out to God for help? When?

PRAYER TIME
Dear God, when the Hebrews cried out for help you heard them and wanted to rescue them. Thank you that you hear me when I talk to you. Amen.

BIBLE TIME
Exodus 3: verses 1-7

God hears

In Midian, Moses had a job looking after sheep in the desert. It was so different from the rich Egyptian Royal Palace!

One day Moses saw a bush burning, and he walked over to it. He heard the voice of God speaking from it.

"I am the God of all your family, Moses," He said. "I have heard my family crying out to Me for help and I want to rescue them from the cruel Egyptians."

Then God said to Moses, "I am sending you to save them, and I will be with you."

Moses was a bit frightened at this, because he didn't think he was good enough to do what God had asked him to do.

TALK TIME
Has there ever been a time that you thought you weren't good enough to do something? Were you a bit frightened?

PRAYER TIME
Dear God, thank you that when you give us a job to do, we will be able to do it because you have given it to us. Help me not to be frightened. Amen.

BIBLE TIME
Exodus 4: verses 10-17

Can't do it

"I can't do it!" said Moses. "I can't... I can't speak very well" he stammered.

God was angry with him and said,

"I will help you. Now leave Midian and return to Egypt!"

God wanted Moses to go and free His family the Hebrews from slavery.

"Take your brother Aaron with you. He will help you," continued God. "Go... for I will be with you, and I will strengthen you."

So Moses and Aaron set off to do the task that God had given them.

TALK TIME
Has there ever been a reason why you couldn't do something? Do you know why?

PRAYER TIME
Dear God, thank you that you gave Moses and Aaron your strength to return to Egypt. Help me to obey you when you tell me to do something. Amen.

BIBLE TIME
Exodus 7: verses 14-16

No... no... no

When Moses and Aaron arrived back in Egypt, they went to see Pharaoh.

God had warned Moses that Pharaoh would not listen to him. Pharaoh did not want Moses' people free from slavery.

Moses asked him, "Let my people go!"

Just as God had said, Pharaoh said "NO!"

Moses went to him again, but still Pharaoh refused to listen and said "NO!" again.

"Don't give up," God said to Moses, and then He told Moses that He would do mighty miracles to free His people from the Egyptians.

TALK TIME
When a person tells you to do something, do you find it hard to listen?

PRAYER TIME
Dear heavenly Father, help me to always listen to you; help me never to be too busy to hear what you want to say to me. Amen

BIBLE TIME
Exodus 8, 9, 10

Plagues

Moses asked Pharaoh again and again to let God's people go, and still he said, "No!"

Then the Lord sent a plague of frogs into Pharaoh's Palace. They hopped all over the place!

Still Pharaoh said, "No!" when Moses asked him to let his people go.

So God sent plagues of flies and gnats and locusts.

Moses went to him again, but still Pharaoh said, "No, I am not letting your people go!"

So God sent a great storm of hail and darkness over the palace. Still Pharaoh said, "No!"

TALK TIME
How do you think Moses felt when Pharaoh kept on saying, "No!"? What did God promise Moses? Look at Day 52.

PRAYER TIME
Dear God, thank you that you stood with Moses all the time he went to Pharaoh. Thank you that you stand with me, too. Amen.

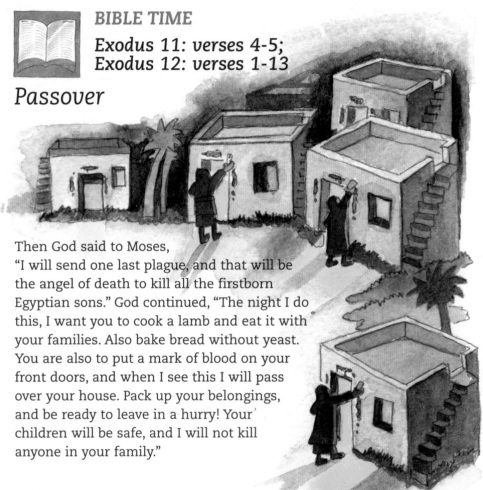

BIBLE TIME
Exodus 11: verses 4-5;
Exodus 12: verses 1-13

Passover

Then God said to Moses,
"I will send one last plague, and that will be
the angel of death to kill all the firstborn
Egyptian sons." God continued, "The night I do
this, I want you to cook a lamb and eat it with
your families. Also bake bread without yeast.
You are also to put a mark of blood on your
front doors, and when I see this I will pass
over your house. Pack up your belongings,
and be ready to leave in a hurry! Your
children will be safe, and I will not kill
anyone in your family."

TALK TIME
*How do you think God's people felt about getting free
from slavery in Egypt? How do you know God was going to
protect them?*

PRAYER TIME
*Dear heavenly Father, thank you that you saved your people, the
Hebrews, and brought them out of Egypt just as you had
planned and promised. Amen.*

BIBLE TIME
Exodus 12: verses 29-32

GO!

God told all of His people to be
ready to leave Egypt during the night.
God had promised them that He
would take them to a very special land.

Just as God had said, at midnight all the Egyptian firstborn
sons in the land were killed.

When the Egyptian children died, there
was much wailing and crying. Pharaoh
called Moses and Aaron and yelled,
"GO, take your people and leave
Egypt... GO and worship your God
who has protected you."

TALK TIME
*How did Pharaoh know that God had protected his people?
Look at Day 54.*

PRAYER TIME
*Dear God, thank you, too, that you protect me and my family.
I ask you that you watch over me today and also during the
night. Amen.*

BIBLE TIME
Exodus 12: verses 34-39

A night-time journey

During the night all of God's people got ready to leave. They wrapped up the bread without yeast. All the parents gathered up the children. They strapped their belongings onto some of their animals.

Then, in the darkness of the night God's people began to leave. They were excited. They knew that God was freeing them from being slaves in Egypt.

TALK TIME
How would you describe being a slave? How do you think the people of God felt when they were set free from slavery?

PRAYER TIME
Dear God, thank you that you freed your people from being slaves. Thank you for the joy you gave them. Amen.

BIBLE TIME
Exodus 14: verses 5-28

Crossing the sea

In Egypt Pharaoh changed his mind about letting God's people go. He rode out after them with troops, chariots, and horsemen to recapture them.

Moses knew that God was with him and said to his people, "Don't be afraid!" As they came to a very big sea, Moses held up his hand, and the sea dried up! All of them were able to cross to the other side safely. What a miracle!

Pharaoh tried to follow them, but the sea rose and crashed onto them. Hooray! Moses and all of God's people had escaped slavery in Egypt.

TALK TIME
God said to Moses, "The Lord will fight for you; you need only to be still." Has there ever been a time when you knew God was on your side?

PRAYER TIME
Dear heavenly Father, when there are times that I am not strong, I know you will stand up for me. Amen.

BIBLE TIME
Exodus 15: verses 1-19

Free at last

After the whole crowd of God's people escaped Pharaoh and his troops, Moses began to sing and dance and praise God:

"I will sing to the Lord, for He is highly exalted,

The Lord is my strength and my song,

He has become my salvation."

TALK TIME
Can you sing a song that praises God?

PRAYER TIME
Dear Lord, I really want to praise you every minute of the day... even when things go wrong I want to praise and sing to you. Amen.

BIBLE TIME

Exodus 20: verses 1-17;
Exodus 34: verses 1 and 35

Wandering

After God's people left Egypt, they wandered in the desert for many years. It was hard for them, but God provided special food for them, called manna, to eat.

God took Moses on top of a mountain, and there He gave him ten rules on two stone tablets. These rules were for God's people to read and obey.

But His people disobeyed these rules and Moses broke the stone tablets. God took Moses again on top of a mountain and gave Moses the same rules on another set of stone tablets.

When Moses left God and came down from the mountain, his face was shining. It shone so much that he had to wear a veil.

TALK TIME

Can you tell by looking at a friend's face that they know God? Why is it different?

PRAYER TIME

Dear God, please help me to try and always keep your rules. Let my face shine because I know you. Amen.

BIBLE TIME
Exodus 25 and 26

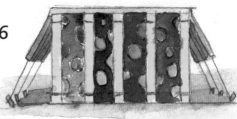

A tabernacle

As God's people wandered in the desert, God spoke to Moses. He told Moses to make a tabernacle so that all of His people would worship Him.

The tabernacle was made of very beautiful colors of purple, red, and blue. Inside the tabernacle was a Holy Place where God told Moses to put a very special box called "The Ark of the Covenant." They were to put the two stones tablets with the rules on them in The Ark. This was to remind the people that the Lord was with them.

TALK TIME
A tabernacle was like a tent. What is your church building like? Is there anything inside the building that reminds you of God?

PRAYER TIME
Dear God, I want to thank you that when I look at................ in my church, it reminds me of you. Amen.

BIBLE TIME

Numbers 13: verses 2 and 17-33

Exploring the land

For forty years God's people wandered through the desert.

Then God said to Moses, "I want you to send out men to go into the new land that I will show you."

So Moses gathered men together, and they went to explore. Forty days later they came back with a huge bunch of big grapes and told the people that the land was indeed beautiful and full of good things.

One of the men said they should take the land, but the rest of them were afraid because the people looked too big and too fierce.

But God told Moses to enter this new land He was giving to them.

TALK TIME

Has there been a time that you have been frightened when something appeared too big for you to do?

PRAYER TIME

Dear Lord, thank you that with you it is possible to do all things. Help me to keep my eyes on you. Amen.

BIBLE TIME
Deuteronomy 34: verses 1-12

A new land

Now God wanted to show Moses the land that He had promised to all of His people. So He took Moses on top of Mount Nebo. There God showed Moses as far as his eyes could see the most beautiful land.

"This land," said God, "is the land that I promised to you and your relatives... Abraham, Isaac, and Jacob. I will give it to you and all of your people forever. But I will not let you, Moses, go into the new land even though you have been special to me... but I will choose another person."

Not long after that, Moses died.

TALK TIME
Having read and learned about Moses, what do you like about him?

PRAYER TIME
Dear heavenly Father, thank you that Moses was a leader of your people and that you gave him strength and wisdom. I pray for strength and wisdom for leaders of our country. Amen.

BIBLE TIME
Joshua 1: verses 1-6

God is with you

After Moses had led his people out of Egypt and they had wandered in the desert for forty years, he died.

God then spoke to Joshua, "Now you will lead my people into the very special land that I have promised you, and I will be with you as you go into this land."

God also said to Joshua, "Be strong! No one will be able to stand up against you... I will always be with you, I will never leave you."

God told Joshua to be brave. He would always be with him and His people.

TALK TIME
Has there ever been a time when you weren't brave but you knew that God was with you? Can you remember when?

PRAYER TIME
Dear heavenly Father, help me always to remember that you will never leave me... especially when I am not feeling brave. Amen.

BIBLE TIME
Joshua 1: verses 10-16

Get ready

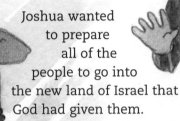

Joshua wanted to prepare all of the people to go into the new land of Israel that God had given them.

"Tell everyone to get ready! Get supplies ready!" Joshua shouted. "We will be crossing the River Jordan in three days."

Joshua told them that they were to help each other across the river into the promised land.

The people replied, "Whatever you tell us to do... we will do. Wherever you say we should go... we will go."

TALK TIME
When you go away somewhere, how do you prepare for the journey?

PRAYER TIME
Dear God, thank you that you told Joshua to prepare his people for traveling, and they wanted to obey his instructions. Amen.

BIBLE TIME
Joshua 2: verses 1-14

Kindness

Before Joshua crossed the River Jordan, he wanted to spy out the land... so he sent out two spies.

The two spies stayed in a city called Jericho with a woman named Rahab.

Now the King of Jericho heard about the two spies and gave orders to his soldiers to find them.

Immediately, Rahab hid the two spies on top of the roof. The soldiers could not find them anywhere. Rahab had saved them!

The two spies promised her that when their people came into land, they would not attack her house because she had hidden the two spies. She was kind.

TALK TIME
Talk about an adventure you have had.

PRAYER TIME
Dear God, thank you that you saved the two spies that Joshua sent out into the land you had promised. Thank you for Rahab's kindness. Amen.

BIBLE TIME
Joshua 3: verses 1-17

A miracle

"I am leading you into the land of Israel," said God. "I will do miracles among you. I will go before you," God continued, "and I will drive out all the enemies in the land."

God also said to them, "When you see the Ark of the Covenant being carried by the priests, stand in the river."

So as the priests entered the water, the people followed them. Then the water stopped flowing, and the river became dry ground. What a miracle! All the people, now called the Israelites, were able to walk across the River Jordan and get across to the other side.

TALK TIME
What was carried in the Ark of the Covenant? Look at Day 60 to find out.

PRAYER TIME
Dear God, thank you for your miracle. Thank you that you saw all of your people safely across the River Jordan. Amen.

BIBLE TIME
Joshua 6: verses 1-5

Be strong

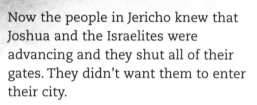

Now the people in Jericho knew that Joshua and the Israelites were advancing and they shut all of their gates. They didn't want them to enter their city.

God told Joshua, "I want all of you to march around the city. Let seven priests blow trumpets in front of the Ark of the Covenant. All of your armed men are to follow the priests. Now do this for seven days."

God then said, "When you hear the priests give a long blast on the trumpets, give a loud SHOUT!"

TALK TIME

What do you think Joshua must have thought about God's instructions? Talk about a time when you felt God was with you, and you had to do something you didn't understand.

PRAYER TIME

Dear heavenly Father, thank you that you told Joshua to be strong and brave. Thank you that I can walk in faith with you. Amen.

BIBLE TIME
Joshua 6: verses 8-25

A promise

Joshua told all the priests and the people to do exactly what God had told him. All the armed men marched. The seven priests blew trumpets while the Ark of the Covenant was carried behind them.

They did this for six days.

On the seventh day they marched around the city seven times, then the trumpeters gave a long blast. "SHOUT NOW!" Joshua yelled. Immediately, all the walls of the city fell down... except Rahab's house, for they had promised that she would be kept safe.

TALK TIME
Why were Rahab and her family kept safe? Look at Day 65.

PRAYER TIME
Dear God, thank you that you always do what you promise. Thank you that you give me promises. Amen.

BIBLE TIME
Joshua 24: verses 11-15

Serve the Lord your God

Joshua wanted to remind the Israelites how God had been with them.

God had brought them out of the land of Egypt, through the desert and crossed the River Jordan and then into the land of Israel... just as He had promised.

Joshua wanted them all to know that God was by their side and had fought all their enemies and defeated them... just as He had promised.

Joshua said to the crowds, "Now fear God. Choose this day to follow the Lord your God. He has been with us all the way." He continued, "As for me and my household, we will serve God."

TALK TIME
Serve means to help... how do you like to help God?

PRAYER TIME
Dear God, teach me to serve you in many ways... I want to follow you wherever you lead me. I know I am safe with you. Amen.

BIBLE TIME
Joshua 24: verses 16-21

God is good

Joshua warned all of the Israelites that they were not to serve any other gods. He reminded them that the Lord had looked after them in many ways... He led them out of slavery from Egypt and performed great miracles in the desert. He protected them on their entire journey to His promised land, Israel. Then He drove out all the enemies in the land so they could enter.

"Never, never go against our God," Joshua said to the people. "He has been SO good to you."

Then all the people shouted back, "We will serve God!"

TALK TIME
Can you say some of the ways that God has been good to you?

PRAYER TIME
Dear heavenly Father, thank you that you go with me to school. Thank you that you give me food to eat. Thank you that I have clothes to wear. Thank you that you go before me. Amen.

BIBLE TIME
Joshua 24: verses 25-27

Keeping a promise

Hearing the people
saying that they
wanted to serve God,
Joshua made a promise that
day that they would always
serve God.

He wrote down in a book
all the laws and rules for
the people to obey. Then he
took a very large stone and
placed it near a tree.

Joshua put the stone in place to
remind the Israelites that they had said
to God, "We will serve you."

TALK TIME
*Have you ever made a promise to God or to friends or family?
Did you keep it?*

PRAYER TIME
*Dear God, help me to keep promises that I make and not to
disappoint friends, family or you. Amen.*

BIBLE TIME

Judges 6: verses 1-6

A broken promise

How sad... after Joshua died the Israelites did not keep their promise to their God.

They did wrong things in His eyes, like worshipping other gods.

God was hurt and sent them some enemies called Midianites. They invaded Israel, camped in the land, ruined the crops, killed the animals, and spoiled the country that God had given to the Israelites.

They felt desperate. They had lost everything. So they began to call out to their God for help.

TALK TIME

Have you ever broken a promise to someone? What happened?

PRAYER TIME

Dear God, if I have ever hurt someone by breaking a promise, please help me to go to them to say sorry. Amen.

BIBLE TIME
Judges 6: verses 7-12

Help

As the people were calling out to God for help, He sent an angel of the Lord to a man called Gideon. At that time Gideon was working hard preparing wheat to be eaten. When the angel invited Gideon to sit down under a tree, the angel said, "The Lord is with you because you are a mighty warrior!"

Gideon looked very surprised and answered, "If the Lord is with us... why has the enemy attacked our land?"

Then the angel reassured Gideon and said, "I am sending you to save my people from their enemies... know that the Lord is with you."

"But Lord," said Gideon, "I am just a poor farmer!"

Again the angel reassured Gideon that the Lord would be with him in the battle against the enemy.

TALK TIME
Sometimes God is called Lord. Talk about how you know God has been with you today.

PRAYER TIME
Dear Lord, I always want to know that you are always with me, especially in difficult times. Amen.

GIDEON

BIBLE TIME
Judges 6: verses 36-38

God speaks

Gideon wanted to fight the enemy that had ruined his land, the land of Israel. But before he did anything, Gideon wanted to know for sure that God had spoken to him. He also wanted to know that God would be there to help him.

So he put out a sheep's fleece on the ground and said to God, "If there is dew on the fleece but not on the ground in the morning, then I will know that you are with me."

The next morning... guess what? There was dew on the fleece but not on the ground!

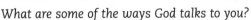

TALK TIME
What are some of the ways God talks to you?

PRAYER TIME
Dear Lord, help me to know for sure that you speak to me and that I will hear you. Amen.

BIBLE TIME
Judges 7: verses 9-15

A dream

Now that Gideon knew for sure that God was with him, he collected an army to battle against the enemy. God spoke again to Gideon and said, "Don't be afraid."

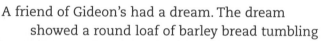

A friend of Gideon's had a dream. The dream showed a round loaf of barley bread tumbling onto the enemy's camp, making all the tents collapse. His friend explained that this was Gideon going into battle against the Midianites, and Gideon's army would win the battle.

When Gideon heard about this dream, he knew that God had spoken to him again. He worshipped God.

TALK TIME
Talk about how God reassures you that He is always there for you.

PRAYER TIME
Dear God, thank you that you are always there to reassure me and to comfort me. Amen.

BIBLE TIME
Judges 7: verses 15-18

God will win

Gideon called his army together. There were only three hundred men in the army. "Get ready!" he said to them. "The Lord God is with us. We will win this battle!" Gideon placed trumpets in their hands and empty jars with lights inside.

"Follow me," he yelled. "When we get to the enemy's camp, blow your trumpets and break the jars!"

"And then," he continued, "I want you to shout 'For the Lord and for Gideon!'" With these instructions the army followed Gideon toward the enemy's camp.

TALK TIME
What do you think the men in the army thought when Gideon told them to take trumpets and jars with lights in them?

PRAYER TIME
Dear Lord God, I am so pleased that you give the right instructions, and you know how to win a battle. Amen.

BIBLE TIME
Joshua 7: verses 19-21

Victory with God

Gideon's army reached the enemy's camp in complete darkness, and they silently surrounded it.

Then Gideon told them to blow hard on their trumpets. The noise was deafening!

They shouted, "For the Lord and for Gideon!"

The enemy was very frightened by the loud noise. They thought that they were being attacked by a HUGE army. They left their camp and ran away a fast as they could!

God had won the battle!

TALK TIME
How does God win battles for you?

PRAYER TIME
Dear God, thank you that you gave Gideon the victory over the enemy. Please have victory in my life when I am having difficult times. Amen.

BIBLE TIME
Joshua 8: verses 28-32

Grateful

The Midianites ran away. Gideon and all of the people of Israel settled back down in the land.

They rebuilt their houses, grew more crops, bred more animals... and everything became peaceful again. The people were so grateful to Gideon.

The peace lasted for quite a few years. The families grew and grew.

Gideon enjoyed the victory that God had given to him and his people. He lived to be a very old age. The people were sad when he died.

TALK TIME
Do you know someone who has died?

PRAYER TIME
Dear heavenly Father, please be with families who have lost loved ones recently. Please comfort all the people in their family. Amen.

BIBLE TIME

1 Samuel 1: verses 1-2 and 12-17

A blessing

There was a man named Elkanah who had two wives. One of the wives had children. The other wife, named Hannah, didn't have any children.

Hannah was very sad about this and cried. One day she went into the temple to pray and to ask God if He would give her a child.

There was a priest in the temple called Eli. He saw that Hannah was upset. He had been watching her pray. As Hannah came out of the temple, Eli gave her a blessing and said, "Go in peace; may God give you what you have asked Him for."

TALK TIME

Say a blessing you have received from God today.

PRAYER TIME

Dear heavenly Father, thank you for all the blessings you give me day by day. Thank you for the blessings you have given me today. Amen.

BIBLE TIME
1 Samuel 1: verses 18-20

Heart's desire

Hannah was delighted that she had received a blessing from Eli, the priest. She smiled. The Lord had heard her. She knew that the Lord was going to give her a baby.

Early the next the morning she arose from her bed to go and worship the Lord in the temple and to thank Him.

Hannah became pregnant and nine months later gave birth to a baby boy. She called him Samuel and said, "Because I asked the Lord for him."

She knew that God had answered her heart's desire for a baby.

TALK TIME
Do you have a heart's desire? Talk about it.

PRAYER TIME
Dear God, thank you for giving Hannah her heart's desire.
I give you my heart's desire today. If it is in your plan for me
I know you will answer it. Amen.

BIBLE TIME
1 Samuel 1: verses 23-28

Giving back...

Elkanah, Hannah's husband, went to the temple to worship the Lord. Hannah stayed at home looking after Samuel. He was a very healthy baby.

Hannah gave thanks to the Lord for giving her such a special baby. In fact she was so grateful that one day she told Elkanah, "I prayed that the Lord would give me a child, and He has. Now I want to give Samuel back to the Lord for whatever plans He has for him."

TALK TIME
What do you like about this story?

PRAYER TIME
Dear Lord, I love the way Hannah gave you back the son you gave her. Help me to give willingly back to you. Amen.

BIBLE TIME
1 Samuel 2: verses 18-21

Wisdom

Hannah thanked God for baby Samuel. She knew that Samuel would serve God in a very special way.

Eli, the priest, taught him many good things about God; Samuel grew up with wisdom.

Each year they traveled to celebrate a special feast in Israel. Each year Hannah made Samuel a beautiful robe to wear.

As time went on, Samuel grew into a young man. God looked upon him with kindness.

TALK TIME
The word "wisdom" means having good sense. Can you talk about sensible things that you have done today?

PRAYER TIME
Dear God, please help me to have your wisdom day by day in all situations. Amen.

BIBLE TIME
1 Samuel 3: verses 1-9

Listening to God

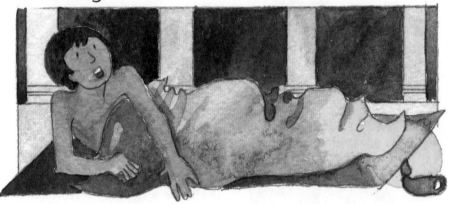

One night Samuel had gone to sleep in the temple near to the Ark of the Covenant. Eli, the priest, was also sleeping not too far away.

During the night the Lord spoke to Samuel. Samuel thought it was Eli calling him. Samuel answered, "Here I am," and he got up and ran to Eli. This happened three times.

Finally, Eli looked at him and said, "I didn't call you. Go back to sleep, and when the Lord calls you again, say that you are listening to Him."

TALK TIME
Can you think about ways of listening to God?

PRAYER TIME
Dear Lord, thank you for Eli's wisdom in Samuel's life. Help me to hear you when you call me. Amen.

BIBLE TIME
1 Samuel 3: verses 11-15

Speak out

The Lord called Samuel again and he replied, "Speak to me Lord, I am listening."

Then God told Samuel that He was about to do something very special in Israel. He also said that Eli's two sons were disobedient. They would never become priests like their father.

The next morning Samuel was afraid to tell Eli all that the Lord had told him, especially the part about his sons.

But Eli called Samuel and said, "Do not hide anything from me. Tell me what the Lord has said to you."

TALK TIME
Have you ever been afraid to speak something out to someone? When?

PRAYER TIME
Dear God, please help me to be strong and not afraid when I need to say something that will help another person. Amen

BIBLE TIME
1 Samuel 3: verses 16-21

Reading the Bible

"Samuel," called Eli, "come here and tell me what the Lord has said to you."

Very bravely, Samuel told Eli all that God had said about Israel, including the part about his two disobedient sons.

"Well," replied Eli. "He is the Lord. His word is final. He must do what is right."

Samuel went on learning all about the Lord by reading the Bible. All of the people in Israel knew that the Lord was with Samuel. They saw that he was a prophet.

TALK TIME
A "prophet" is God's messenger who tells people of His will. Samuel read his Bible so that he would know God. How often do you read your Bible?

PRAYER TIME
Dear God, help me to read my Bible more to learn and know about you... just like Samuel. Amen.

BIBLE TIME
1 Samuel 8: verses 6-10

Dishonest

When Samuel was very old, his sons became men of the law. They also became very dishonest.

The people were upset about this and came to Samuel and said, "We want a king for Israel!"

They also said to him, "All the other countries have kings... we want one, too."

Samuel became unhappy. He prayed to God for an answer.

"Listen to the people and give them a king," God said. "There is a man called Saul. He will be made king and lead the people of Israel."

TALK TIME
Dishonest means not being fair. What do you think about Samuel's sons?

PRAYER TIME
Dear Lord, when I am unhappy just like Samuel... I want to come to you and pray. I know you will always have an answer. Amen.

BIBLE TIME
1 Samuel 9: verses 21-25;
1 Samuel 10: verse 1

A leader and a king

When Samuel met Saul, he told him that he would be the first king of Israel.

Saul was amazed. "How can this be? I am from such a small tribe, and we are not important at all."

Samuel reassured Saul that he would be the king.

Then Samuel brought Saul to his home where all his servants were gathered. They all sat down together for a meal.

It was a very special occasion. Samuel had already prepared food to eat. It was fit for a king!

After the meal the two men talked together on the roof.

TALK TIME
Can you talk about the food that God provides for you?

PRAYER TIME
Dear God, thank you for all the food you give us, and best of all thank you for............ which I love to eat! Amen.

BIBLE TIME
1 Samuel 13: verses 7-13

Wait

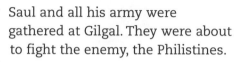

Saul and all his army were gathered at Gilgal. They were about to fight the enemy, the Philistines.

Samuel had asked Saul to wait for him before going into battle. Samuel had promised to burn a sacrifice for Saul and the troops before they fought the Philistines.

Saul waited and waited and waited for Samuel... but he didn't arrive.

So Saul impatiently decided to go ahead and burn the sacrifice without him. A little while later Samuel arrived. "What have you done?" he asked. "You acted foolishly. You haven't kept the Lord's orders."

TALK TIME
Are you ever impatient when you have been told to wait for something?

PRAYER TIME
Dear Lord, help me to always be patient and wait for you and not go ahead of you. Amen.

BIBLE TIME
1 Samuel 15: verses 7-10

Turned away

God made Saul the king. He won many battles. The people cheered that they had such a good leader. Saul also chose his son Jonathan to head up some of his troops. Jonathan was very brave and won many battles, too.

But when Saul won a battle, he didn't obey God. He stole many of the animals belonging to the enemy. God had told him not to.

The Lord spoke to Samuel, "I am so sad that I have made Saul the king. He has turned away from me."

TALK TIME
Do you know of anyone who has turned against God? What would you say to that person?

PRAYER TIME
Dear God, help me to speak to people who need to turn back to you. Amen.

BIBLE TIME
1 Samuel 15: verses 12-20

Don't blame

Samuel was very worried that Saul, the king, had disobeyed God. So early next morning Samuel went to meet him. King Saul greeted him and said, "The Lord bless you. I have carried out God's instructions when we went to battle."

Samuel pointed to the animals that King Saul had taken from the enemy and said, "Why have you disobeyed God and taken these animals from the enemy when He told you not to?"

"I didn't take them... it was my troops," stammered King Saul. But Saul knew he was blaming the troops for the things that he had done wrong.

TALK TIME
Has anyone ever blamed you for something they did wrong? What happened?

PRAYER TIME
Dear God, please forgive us when we blame other people when we know it's our fault. Amen.

BIBLE TIME
1 Samuel 15: verses 20-26

Sorry

"But I did obey the Lord," said King Saul to Samuel. "I went on a mission and completely destroyed all of the enemies. We took the best of their animals to make sacrifices to the Lord. We only wanted to give the best to the Lord."

Then Samuel said, "The Lord would prefer your obedience rather than your wrong giving. You have not listened to the Lord. You have done wrong." Samuel continued, "The Lord is sorry that he chose you to be the king. He has decided to look for a new king to replace you."

King Saul was so sorry and begged for forgiveness.

TALK TIME
Has there been a time that you had to say sorry to someone? What happened?

PRAYER TIME
Dear Lord, please help me to say the right words when I go to someone to say sorry. Amen.

BIBLE TIME
1 Samuel 16: verses 1-10

A new king

Samuel was sad that King Saul had been bad. One day the Lord told Samuel, "I want you to take some oil, for I am going to send you to Bethlehem, and there I will show you the man I have chosen to be the next king of Israel."

The Lord also said to him that He would choose a man whose heart would be right towards Him.

The Lord led Samuel to a family. The father's name was Jesse. He lined up seven of his sons for Samuel to see who would be the next king.

But Samuel knew in his heart none of them was God's chosen one.

TALK TIME
In your heart how do you feel about God?

PRAYER TIME
Dear Lord, please let my heart always love you. Amen.

BIBLE TIME
1 Samuel 16: verses 11-13

He is the one!

"Have you got any other sons?" Samuel asked Jesse, the father.

Samuel knew that none of the seven sons standing in front of him was chosen to be the next king of Israel.

Jesse told Samuel that there was one more son who was looking after the sheep on the hillside.

"Please go and get him," asked Samuel.

A little while later they returned with the one son who had been looking after the sheep. As soon as Samuel saw him, the Lord told Samuel, "That is the one I have chosen."

So Samuel poured oil on the head of the son called David and anointed him king over Israel.

TALK TIME
How do you know God has chosen you?

PRAYER TIME
Dear God, thank you that I have been chosen by you for a special plan. Amen.

BIBLE TIME
1 Samuel 16: verses 14-23

David plays

Now King Saul was very unhappy. He had turned away from God. One day King Saul said to his servants, "Find someone who can soothe me when I am being tormented. Find someone who can play the harp for me and sing."

One of the servants replied, "I know! The son of Jesse in Bethlehem! He plays the harp well and also is a brave man of God."

So David was sent for and lived in King Saul's palace.

Whenever King Saul felt miserable, David would play the harp for him.

TALK TIME

Can you play an instrument? What tune do you like playing on it? Can you sing? Can you sing a song to the Lord?

PRAYER TIME

Dear Heavenly Father, thank you for David who soothed King Saul with his music. Amen.

BIBLE TIME
1 Samuel 17: verses 1-11

A big GIANT!

Fierce fighting was going on between King Saul and the Philistines.

In the Philistine army there was a fighter called Goliath... he was a GIANT of a man and towered above everyone! He wore the most incredible armor which was very heavy. He was very frightening to look at.

One day Goliath, the giant, shouted out across to King Saul's army, "Choose a man to fight me, and I will kill him for sure!"

All of the men in King Saul's army were terrified and scared!

TALK TIME
Has there ever been a time that you have felt scared? What happened?

PRAYER TIME
Dear God, please help me when I am scared of something. When I am scared, I want to know you are by my side. Amen.

BIBLE TIME
1 Samuel 17: verses 12-20

Food supplies

Three of David's brothers were in King Saul's army fighting against the Philistines.

One day, Jesse, David's father, suggested to David that he take food supplies to his brothers. So David collected some loaves of bread and roasted grain for his brothers. He also brought some cheese for the rest of the leaders in the army.

He left his flock of sheep, put the food parcel on his donkey, and went on his way to find his brothers fighting in the army.

TALK TIME
Do you think it would be fun to cook something for somebody and give it to them? Who would help you cook?

PRAYER TIME
Dear God, thank you that you supply us with food to share with others. Amen.

103

BIBLE TIME
1 Samuel 17: verses 23-32

David hears the giant

When David arrived at the battleground, he left the food with the food supply keeper and greeted his brothers. While David talked with them, he heard a roar, "Find a man who will fight me, and I will kill him!"

It was Goliath, the giant, shouting across from the Philistine army to King Saul's army.

Again everyone in King Saul's army became frightened. David asked, "Who is this man? Who is this man that defies the living God?"

Some men in the army told David that King Saul would give great wealth to whoever defeated the giant Goliath.
"I'll kill him!" said David.

TALK TIME
Bravery means being bold and having courage. Talk about a time when you felt brave.

PRAYER TIME
Dear Lord, I know when there are times that I need to feel extra brave. Please be with me in these times. Amen.

BIBLE TIME
1 Samuel 17: verses 28-33

Don't be so silly

"What, YOU kill the giant?!" said David's brother. "You're FAR too young to kill a giant... why, you've only come to watch the battle. Don't be so SILLY! Besides, you're being too cocky to think you could tackle this giant Goliath."

These were the words that David's brother yelled at him, but David was sure that he could kill the giant. When King Saul heard that David was brave enough to fight Goliath, he asked David to go to the palace.

"You.... fight the giant?! No never," shouted King Saul. "Goliath is FAR too big for you to kill. You are just a boy!"

TALK TIME
Has anyone ever said that you can't do something, but you know that you can? How did you feel?

PRAYER TIME
Dear heavenly Father, thank you for David's courage and bravery. I want to know that you give me boldness to do things for you, too. Amen.

BIBLE TIME
1 Samuel 17: verses 34-37

With God's strength

When David heard King Saul say that he couldn't kill Goliath, he replied, "For many years I have looked after my father's sheep day and night. When a bear or a lion comes to kill one of the lambs I fight them off... I've tackled these animals and killed them. I can surely kill this giant."

David continued, "I am not frightened."

King Saul looked at David. "Go," he said, "and may the Lord be with you."

TALK TIME
When someone has to face a difficult situation, have you ever said to them, "May the Lord go with you"?

PRAYER TIME
Dear Lord, help me to encourage my friends. Help us to know that if we turn to you... you will walk with us. Amen.

BIBLE TIME
1 Samuel 17: verses 39-40

No armor

King Saul put his own armor and helmet on David, and he fastened his sword around David's waist. King Saul knew David would need to be well protected!

But David wasn't used to being dressed in such heavy protective clothing. He tried walking around in them to get used to it. It felt very funny.

"I can't fight Goliath in this!" said David.

So he took it all off and stood in his linen tunic. Then he chose five smooth stones from a stream and put them in a pouch along with his sling.

Now he felt more at ease and ready to kill the giant!

TALK TIME
What clothes do you feel comfortable in and why?

PRAYER TIME
Dear Lord, thank you that David had peace to fight the enemy and knew you would go before him. Amen.

BIBLE TIME
1 Samuel 17: verses 40-44

Fight me!

David marched out to meet the giant Goliath. The giant was dressed in full armor and ready for battle.

Goliath saw David coming toward him and looked down on him. He saw that David was very little compared to him. He also saw that David was healthy and handsome, and he didn't like him.

"Hey," said Goliath. "So you've come to fight me. Well, I hate your God and hate you. You're crazy to think you can kill me with only a stick! I'll kill you instantly."

David looked, and listened to Goliath. He wasn't frightened of Goliath's boasting at all.

TALK TIME
Have you ever listened to someone boasting? What did they say? How did you feel?

PRAYER TIME
Dear Lord, help me never to boast to other people about what I can do. Amen.

BIBLE TIME
1 Samuel 17: verses 45-49

It's the Lord's battle

David waited until Goliath had finished his boasting. Then David said, "You may have all the top kind of armor with all the right kind of swords and spears to kill me with, but I have to tell you that I come against you in the name of the Lord, the God of the armies of Israel."

Goliath laughed at David! "How can a mere boy hurt me?" he thought. "Who does he think he is?"

David stood still and took one of the stones out of his pouch and put it in the sling. With God by his side he was ready to fight.

TALK TIME
Mention a time when you knew that God fought for you in a difficult situation.

PRAYER TIME
Dear heavenly Father, thank you that when I pray to you to fight for me in difficult situations, you also protect me. Amen.

BIBLE TIME
1 Samuel 17: verses 49-51

The enemy is killed

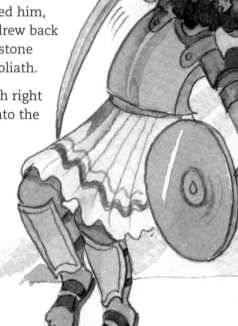

As the big giant approached him, David was very calm. He drew back the sling and WHAM, the stone flew into the air toward Goliath.

The small stone hit Goliath right on his forehead. He fell onto the ground with a loud thud.

David killed the enemy with just one stone!

When the Philistine army saw this, they all turned and fled.

David was a hero!

TALK TIME
When you have had a difficult time, how God has helped you through it?

PRAYER TIME
Dear God, thank you that you give us the victory when we fight in your name. Amen.

BIBLE TIME
1 Samuel 18: verses 1-4

Friends forever

King Saul had a son named Jonathan. David loved Jonathan and became his best friend. They spoke often together and enjoyed one another's company.

They both shared adventures in battle and in winning wars. They had lots to talk about.

One day Jonathan wanted to show David just how much he valued their wonderful friendship, so he gave David his cloak, tunic, sword, bow, and belt.

TALK TIME
Have you ever given to a friend something that belongs to you because you love them? What did you give?

PRAYER TIME
Dear Lord, you always love a cheerful giver... teach me to give something away today. Amen.

DAVID AND KING SAUL *Day 105*

BIBLE TIME
1 Samuel 18: verses 6-9

Jealousy

Whatever King Saul gave to David to do, David did it well and successfully. When all the army and King Saul returned from battle after killing Goliath, everyone cheered, clapped, danced, and sang.

Hooray! David, the shepherd boy, had killed the big giant.

As they danced through the streets, King Saul saw that all the people liked David much more than him. He also knew that the Lord was with David. He became jealous.

TALK TIME

"Jealousy" means wanting something that others have. When you have been jealous?

PRAYER TIME

Dear God, please help me when I feel jealous. Let me know that the best thing ever to have is you. Amen.

BIBLE TIME
1 Samuel 19: verses 1-18

King Saul is angry

King Saul told his son Jonathan that he wanted to kill David. Jonathan tried to talk his father out of it. He told him just how good David was. He tried to explain that killing him wouldn't be the right thing to do.

King Saul listened and then said, "All right then, David will live!"

Jonathan went to look for David and brought him back into the palace. Once more David played his harp for the king. But after a while King Saul became jealous of David again and tried to kill him.

David fled from the palace and ran until he reached the prophet, Samuel, who hid him from King Saul.

TALK TIME
What was David like?

PRAYER TIME
Dear Lord, you said that David had a heart for you. Teach me also to have a heart for you like David. Amen.

BIBLE TIME
2 Samuel 5: verses 1-3

David becomes king

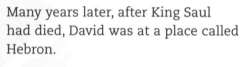

Many years later, after King Saul had died, David was at a place called Hebron.

"You are the one that has led us in war," the people shouted.

"We have seen that the Lord is with you! We know that you are a shepherd who will become our king!" they said.

On that day David made a promise with them that he would be responsible and rule over them all.

Then David became king of Israel.

TALK TIME
Who first anointed David as King? Look at Day 93.

PRAYER TIME
Dear God, it's so good that you have a very special plan for my life, just like you did for David. Amen.

BIBLE TIME
2 Samuel 5: verses 6-10

Jerusalem

How proud all the people were that David was their new king.

One day King David marched toward Jerusalem. This city had been taken over by some enemies, but now David wanted it for himself and his family

King David and his army fought and won against the enemies in Jerusalem. David moved into the city and built his home there. He called it "The city of David." He built up the walls around the houses. Jerusalem looked very grand and well protected!

King David became stronger and stronger because God was with him.

TALK TIME
How do you know that God is with you?

PRAYER TIME
Dear Lord, thank you that you are walking by my side all the time. Amen.

BIBLE TIME
2 Samuel 5: verses 17-25

Ask the Lord

In the land of Israel there was an enemy called the Philistines. The Philistines heard that David had been made king, and they wanted to attack him. David heard this news and he asked the Lord, "Shall I go and fight the enemy?"

God heard David and He answered, "GO." David fought the enemy and won the battle. Once more the Philistines approached David and his army to fight. King David asked God again, "Shall I go and fight the enemy?" God told David to go again and fight, and even told David how to win the battle.

TALK TIME
Do you ever ask the Lord how to do something?

PRAYER TIME
Help me, dear Lord, to always ask you before I go and do something so that I may hear your right instructions. Amen.

BIBLE TIME
2 Samuel 6: verses 3-12

The ark

King David wanted to bring the Ark of the Covenant up to the city of Jerusalem. He ordered a new cart to be built, and then he went to collect it from the house where it was being kept.

King David and friends put the Ark of the Covenant onto the cart. They began to take it very carefully towards the city of Jerusalem.

On the way, King David and all his family danced and danced and played many musical instruments. They were happy to have the Ark of the Covenant back with them.

TALK TIME
The Ark of the Covenant was very special because it reminded the people of God. David danced before the Ark... do you like to dance for the Lord, too?

PRAYER TIME
Let me dance before you Lord... let me dance with joy because I love you. Amen.

BIBLE TIME
2 Samuel 7: verses 1-29

Future plans

God had given King David a beautiful palace, but David said, "This isn't right. Here I am in a wonderful palace and yet the Ark of the Covenant remains in a tent!"

So God sent a man called Nathan, a prophet, who said to David, "One day the Lord will build a very special place to put the Ark of the Covenant... however, it won't be you who will build it but another person in your family."

David began to thank God for letting him know of His great plan to build a special place to put the Ark. He thanked Him, too, for his family and for the land of Israel.

TALK TIME
Have you got plans for your life? Share them.

PRAYER TIME
Dear Lord, I'm so glad that you know my plans... it gives me such peace that you are in control. Amen.

BIBLE TIME
2 Samuel 11: verses 1-3

King David does wrong

It was spring, and all of King David's army were fighting the enemies... but David stayed at home in Jerusalem.

One evening, after supper, David went on top of the palace roof and walked around. It was peaceful.

He glanced across the rooftops and saw a beautiful woman named Bathsheba.

Now Bathsheba was already married. For David to look at and long for another man's wife was sinful in God's eyes.

TALK TIME
Do you know what sinful means?

PRAYER TIME
Dear Lord, how wonderful you are that you know when we do things wrong and yet you forgive us. Amen.

BIBLE TIME

2 Samuel 11: verse 15;
2 Samuel 12: verses 13-16 and 24-25

David asks for forgiveness

King David had done wrong in God's eyes. Not only had he looked at another man's wife but also he gave an order for Bathsheba's husband to be killed. David and Bathsheba had a baby, but the baby died.

One day Nathan, the prophet, came to King David and said, "The Lord made you king over all Israel and He gave you so much... but you misused His kindness and have sinned."

When King David heard Nathan say all of this, he became so sorry that he had sinned.

He married Bathsheba and they had another baby. They named the baby Solomon.

TALK TIME

What do you do after you have done something wrong?

PRAYER TIME

Dear Lord, I am so sorry that I upset you sometimes. Please forgive me. Amen.

BIBLE TIME
2 Samuel 22: verses 1-51

David is thankful

King David was thankful to God for all that He had given him.

David loved God with all of his heart and knew that God had helped him win many battles. Even when he had sinned, he knew that God had forgiven him. And the Lord loved David, too.

One day David sat down and sang a song to God to thank Him.

The words of this song are, "You are my rock, Lord, you are a hiding place for me, you are so worthy Lord and I praise your name. You train my hands for battle, and you set me free..."

TALK TIME
Sing a song that praises the Lord.

PRAYER TIME
Dear Lord, I always want to sing a song to you!
I am so thankful for all that you have done for me. Amen.

BIBLE TIME
1 Chronicles 22: verses 1-5

Preparing for the temple

"The Lord is going to build a temple," said King David to the people in Jerusalem, "and we need to prepare for it now!"

Iron was made into nails, bronze was shipped into Israel, beautiful wood was delivered – everything was supplied to start building.

King David gathered together gatekeepers and priests who would take care of his people.
He called musicians and singers together, waiting to play and sing in the new temple.

TALK TIME
Look at a map and find out where Jerusalem is.
What do you like about your own church building?

PRAYER TIME
Dear Lord, thank you that you provided us with a wonderful place to worship you. Amen.

BIBLE TIME
1 Chronicles 22: verses 6-12

Preparing for the temple

King David was very busy with the preparations for the temple. He said, "I have taken every care to see to it that this temple will be special, but I will not be building it... the person who will build it is my son, Solomon."

So David called his son and said to him, "The Lord has told me that you will be the man to build the special house for everyone to worship in. But," continued King David, "you must obey the Lord in all things."

TALK TIME
What happens when you forget to obey God?

PRAYER TIME
Dear Lord, please help me to be good and follow you. Amen.

BIBLE TIME
1 Kings 1: verses 38-40

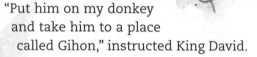

A new king

King David called together Nathan, the prophet, a priest, and others and sent them to get his son Solomon.

"Put him on my donkey and take him to a place called Gihon," instructed King David.

So the men went and did just as King David had asked. Then the priest took some oil and poured it on Solomon's head, anointing the new king of Israel.

"Praise the Lord!" shouted the people. "Long live King Solomon!" Then they blew trumpets very loudly in celebration.

TALK TIME

What other king of Israel was anointed in this way? Look at Day 93.
Name a special occasion. How do you celebrate it?

PRAYER TIME

Dear Lord, you love us to celebrate your goodness. Help me always to include you in celebrations. Amen.

BIBLE TIME
1 Kings 2: verses 1-12

Son Solomon

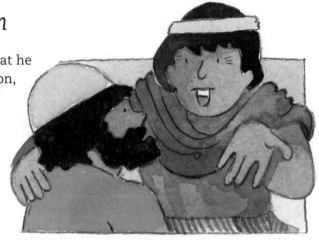

King David knew that he was going to die soon, so he called for his son Solomon. He wanted to pass on some good advice.

"Always walk with the Lord your God," King David said. "And always walk with Him with all of your heart and soul. You must show kindness. Let people eat at your dining table and show them respect. Always deal with things with great wisdom, my son."

Not long after, King David died. His son Solomon sat on the throne of Israel and became the new king of Israel.

TALK TIME
If you could give advice to someone, what would you say?

PRAYER TIME
Dear God, thank you that you loved King David and that he loved you. Thank you for his good advice. Amen.

BIBLE TIME
1 Kings 3: verses 2-14

Asking for wisdom

King Solomon showed his love to God by following all His rules. He made sacrifices of thanks to God in many different places.

One night King Solomon was sleeping, and the Lord appeared to him in a dream.

"Ask for whatever you want," God said to him.

"O Lord," said King Solomon, "you have chosen me to be a king and I will be your servant. I am reigning over many people in Israel... so please give me wisdom."

"I will give you much wisdom," replied the Lord, "and as you haven't asked for anything else, I will also give you great wealth."

TALK TIME
Solomon was given godly wisdom. Would you like to have this from God?

PRAYER TIME
Dear God, may I ask today for your wisdom in all that I do and say? Amen.

BIBLE TIME
1 Kings 4: verses 20-34

Abundance from God

God blessed King Solomon! He gave him and his people numerous cattle, sheep, and goats. There was plenty to eat for everyone.

In King Solomon's stables there were forty thousand horses... that's a lot!

Trees produced grapes and figs. And all tables everywhere were full of food.

Just as God had promised, He gave King Solomon great wisdom to rule his people.

King Solomon taught different wise sayings, he sang songs, and taught about plants, animals, birds, and fish.

Many people from many different countries came to listen to King Solomon because of his wisdom.

TALK TIME
What teacher at school do you like to learn from and why?

PRAYER TIME
Dear God, thank you for teachers at school and for their wisdom in teaching me. Amen.

BIBLE TIME
1 Kings 5: verses 13-18

Solomon builds the temple

Now was the special time to build the first temple in Jerusalem. King Solomon wanted this building to be the very best for God.

He hired men who could build, men who could saw wood, and carpenters who could carve special doors. There was gold and silver on the columns, colorful decorations on the walls.

Everyone worked very hard building the temple. They all gave their best. They hammered, sawed, polished, painted, carved, and decorated.

All in all, it took the workers seven years to finish the temple. It looked so beautiful!

TALK TIME
How can you give your best when you do something for God?

PRAYER TIME
Dear Lord, help me to give my best when I do something for you. I know this will please you. Amen.

BIBLE TIME
1 Kings 7: verses 48-51

Inside the temple

King Solomon then had all the men make special ornaments to put inside the temple so that all the priests and the people could worship the Lord. There was a golden altar, a golden table for the altar bread, lampstands, and an altar that gave off a perfume that sent prayers up to Heaven.

King Solomon built a special place inside of the temple. It was called the "Holy of Holies."

He then gathered his men together for the most important task – to collect the Ark of the Covenant and bring it into the temple.

When it was placed in the "Holy of Holies", all the people knew that God was with them.

TALK TIME

Holy means pure and godly. Say ways you enjoy worshipping a Holy God.

PRAYER TIME

Dear Lord, I love to come and worship you. I love to dance and sing just for you. You are a Holy God! Amen.

BIBLE TIME
1 Kings 10: verses 1-13

Queen of Sheba

There was a queen who lived far away and had heard about King Solomon. So one day she packed up lots of gold, spices, and precious stones on her camels and set off to meet King Solomon. She wanted to ask him some questions and to test his wisdom. When she arrived in Jerusalem, the queen was overwhelmed by his wealth! When she asked some tricky questions, King Solomon answered each with great wisdom.

"You are indeed as wise and wealthy as I have heard," she said to him. "God has indeed blessed you as King of Israel." Then the Queen of Sheba gave all her gold, spices, and precious stones as presents to King Solomon.

TALK TIME
When someone asks you questions, do you ask for God's wisdom on how to answer?

PRAYER TIME
Dear God, thank you for the wisdom you gave King Solomon. Help me to answer my friends the way you want me to. Don't let me talk foolishly. Amen.

BIBLE TIME
1 Kings 11: verses 1-13

King Solomon disobeys

God blessed Solomon. As the years went by, King Solomon became richer and richer and wiser and wiser. The whole earth came to Jerusalem to see him and they all presented gifts to him.

However, King Solomon began to disobey God. He married several foreign women who led the king away from God. His wives also led him away from God by worshipping idols.

"You have disobeyed me and I am angry," said the God of Israel to King Solomon. "Now I will take away many of the things I have given you and, what's more, your son, the next king, will not be as rich as you."

TALK TIME
"Idols" means things that people worship instead of God. Can you name some of the idols people worship today?

PRAYER TIME
Dear God, help me to worship only you, today and forever more. Amen.

BIBLE TIME
1 Kings 17: verses 1 and 7

Special messenger

There were many kings after King Solomon who ruled over Israel. Some were good and some were bad.

There was one king, King Ahab, who was very bad and instead of worshipping God, he worshipped golden idols.

So God called a man named Elijah, a prophet, to go and warn King Ahab that there would be no rain in the next few years.

This was God's way of making King Ahab see that he was doing wrong and was doing great harm to the people.

And so, just as God had said, the rain stopped in the land of Israel.

TALK TIME
Do you know what happens when it doesn't rain for a long time?

PRAYER TIME
Dear Lord, thank you so much that you send rain on our land so that seeds and plants can grow... and I can wash! Amen.

BIBLE TIME
1 Kings 17: verses 2-6

God provides

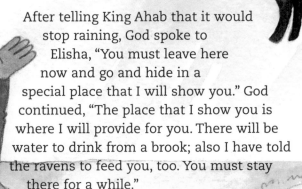

After telling King Ahab that it would stop raining, God spoke to Elisha, "You must leave here now and go and hide in a special place that I will show you." God continued, "The place that I show you is where I will provide for you. There will be water to drink from a brook; also I have told the ravens to feed you, too. You must stay there for a while."

Elijah found this special place and rested. Then the ravens brought him bread and meat, and he drank clear, pure water from the brook.

TALK TIME
Besides going to bed to rest... where else do you like to take a rest?

PRAYER TIME
Dear Lord, thank you that you are with me even when I am resting. It's so good to know that you watch over me always. Amen.

BIBLE TIME
1 Kings 17: verses 7-9

No rain

After Elijah had spoken to King Ahab... not one drop of rain fell from the sky!

The rivers dried up, plants didn't grow, and people had little food to eat.

Then God spoke to Elijah again, "Go and find a woman, who is a widow, in a town that I will show you. I have told her to look after you and to feed you. She will provide you with all that you need to eat."

So Elijah set off. He trusted God to provide for him, as there was a famine in the land of Israel.

TALK TIME
The word "famine" means severe shortage of food.
Do you know of a country which has a famine at the moment?

PRAYER TIME
Dear God, thank you for showing me about this country.
Please provide in a very special way for all of the people who don't have food. Amen.

BIBLE TIME
1 Kings 17: verses 10-12

No food

So Elijah set off to find the widow that God had told him about. A little later, after walking some distance he arrived at the gates of a town and saw a woman gathering sticks. Then God showed Elijah that this was the woman to help him.

He called out to the woman, "Please, is it possible you could give me a drink? Also, do you have some bread for me to eat?"

She looked up at Elijah and replied, "I don't have any bread. My son and I are so hungry. I am gathering these sticks to make a fire and cook the last bit of bread we have in the house... and then we will die of starvation."

TALK TIME
Have you ever thought about giving money to people in other countries who don't have much food?

PRAYER TIME
Dear God, please take care of all those who do not have food. Please, dear God, help me to help them. Amen.

BIBLE TIME
1 Kings 17: verses 13-16

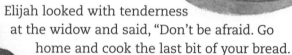

Giving away

Elijah looked with tenderness at the widow and said, "Don't be afraid. Go home and cook the last bit of your bread. Make me a small piece of bread and then make some for yourself and your son."

Elijah knew that God would provide for her.

The widow went away and did just as Elijah had told her. In her kitchen she mixed the last bit of flour and oil together... but every time she emptied the jars of oil and flour, the jars filled up again! This was another miracle from God.

Finally, when the bread was cooked, she gave a piece to Elijah.

Each day after that she found that there was enough oil and flour left over to provide for her and her son until it rained again.

TALK TIME

As the widow gave to Elijah so God blessed her. Have you ever found that if you give something away God blesses you?

PRAYER TIME

Dear God, thank you for providing for Elijah and the widow during the famine. Thank you for blessing the widow and her son. Amen.

BIBLE TIME
1 Kings 18: verses 16-18

Who's the troublemaker?

After a while, King Ahab wanted to meet Elijah. He remembered that it was Elijah who had said that there wouldn't be any rain in Israel for a few years. Now, just as he had said, the whole of the land of Israel had dried up, and there was indeed a great famine.

When he saw Elijah he pointed his finger at him and said, "You're a troublemaker here."

"No, I'm not," replied Elijah. "But you and your family have brought trouble. You have disobeyed God's laws and have worshipped other idols. This has saddened the God of Israel."

TALK TIME
What things in the world today make God sad?

PRAYER TIME
Dear God, I am so sorry that you are sad when we do things wrong today in our world. Please forgive us. Amen.

BIBLE TIME
1 Kings 18: verses 19-21

A contest

Elijah looked at King Ahab and said, "I want you to gather 450 of your prophets who worship false gods. I will meet them on Mount Carmel for a contest."

So King Ahab sent word out to all of his prophets that they were to meet Elijah.

It was going to be 450 false prophets against one true man of God!

Elijah instructed the false prophets to lay a bull on a big fire, and he would do the same. But they weren't allowed to light the fire...

TALK TIME
Whose side is God on and why?

PRAYER TIME
Dear God, thank you that you are so powerful and always have the victory for us. Amen.

BIBLE TIME
1 Kings 18: verses 24-26

No fire!

"Now," said Elijah, "the contest is to see whose god will set the wood on fire!" So the 450 prophets from King Ahab's side collected a bull... so did Elijah. The other prophets collected wood... so did Elijah.

Then the prophets began to call on their god to light the wood. They called and they called and they called. There was such a noise on Mount Carmel! They danced around the wood, they shouted to their god, but still the wood didn't light.

"Shout louder!" mocked Elijah, "Perhaps your god didn't hear you!" But still the wood didn't burn.

TALK TIME
Elijah stood alone against 450 who didn't believe in his God. Is it sometimes hard for you to stand alone for God?

PRAYER TIME
Dear God, help me to stand up for you and be brave. Help me to talk about you to others. Amen.

BIBLE TIME
1 Kings 18: verses 30-39

Fire from Heaven!

"Come here!" said Elijah to all of King Ahab's prophets. "Come here to my altar and cut up my bull." So they did.

"Now," he said, "pour water on my wood." And they did. Elijah asked them to do it three more times. And they did. Then Elijah prayed to the God of Israel.

"God, send your power from heaven," he shouted. Immediately fire fell and burned up all of his wood and the bull, even though it was very wet from the water.

The false prophets stood back in amazement.

When they saw Elijah's wood burst into flames, they all believed in the God of Israel.

TALK TIME
Why do you think Elijah wanted God to send fire from heaven?

PRAYER TIME
Dear God, I'm always amazed at your miracles that make other people believe in you. Amen.

BIBLE TIME
1 Kings 18: verses 42-45

Rain at last!

After God had shown His power to the 450 false prophets, Elijah climbed to the top of Mount Carmel. He took a servant with him and said to him, "Go and look toward the sea."

The servant did as he was told and came back to Elijah.

"I see nothing," he said.

Seven times Elijah told him to look. On the seventh time the servant come back and told him, "There is a very small cloud in the sky."

"Quickly now," said Elijah, "go and tell King Ahab before it pours with rain."

Then the sky gradually turned black, and it began to pour with rain in Israel! God had kept his promise!

TALK TIME
Look back at Day 125 and see why there wasn't any rain for a few years in the land of Israel.

PRAYER TIME
Dear God, thank you for Elijah telling King Ahab what would happen to him when he worshipped other gods. Amen.

BIBLE TIME
1 Kings 19: verses 19-20

Elijah finds Elisha

God spoke to Elijah. He told him to go and meet a man called Elisha. This young man would succeed him as a prophet.

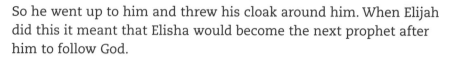

So Elijah set off to find Elisha. He found him busy plowing a field. Elijah knew immediately that this was the man that God had spoken about.

So he went up to him and threw his cloak around him. When Elijah did this it meant that Elisha would become the next prophet after him to follow God.

Elisha knew what was happening. He left his cattle and plow and followed Elijah.

TALK TIME
What do you like about Elisha and why?

PRAYER TIME
Dear Lord, help me to follow you wherever you take me... just like Elisha. Amen.

BIBLE TIME
1 Kings 12

Many bad kings

During this time in Israel, many kings ruled over the people. Most of them worshipped other gods and not the God of Israel, which made the people do wrong things and sin against the God.

One king, Jehu, worshipped a golden calf. Another king, King Rehoboam, forgot God's laws. God let the Egyptians take away all the people's treasures.

Many kings in Israel disobeyed God and the people were led astray.

TALK TIME
What happens if you follow a bad person?

PRAYER TIME
Dear Lord, help me to follow all the good things that you teach me. Help me to follow friends that know you. Amen.

BIBLE TIME
2 Kings 22: verses 1-2

Some good kings

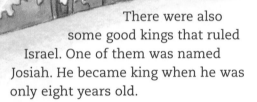

There were also some good kings that ruled Israel. One of them was named Josiah. He became king when he was only eight years old.

King Josiah loved God with all his heart.

He saw that the people of Israel had very wicked ways. This upset him, and he tore his clothes and wept before God. He knew that God was angry with all of His people for disobeying Him.

King Josiah repaired the temple so the people of Israel could worship. He read all of God's laws to them.

Gradually, everyone turned back to God because of the good king, Josiah.

TALK TIME
Talk about following good people. What happens?

PRAYER TIME
Dear God, please give us good leaders for our country, ones that know your laws and rules. Amen.

BIBLE TIME
2 Kings 2: verses 1-12

Elisha's desire

Elijah and Elisha were leaving a place called Gilgal. Elijah said to Elisha, "Stay here for a while because I am going onto Bethel."

But Elisha said, "No, I won't leave you. I want to go with you."

So they traveled together.

Now Elijah knew that God was about to take him home to heaven, so he said to Elisha, "What can I do for you?"

Elisha answered, "I would like to follow God just as you have done."

Elijah then said to Elisha, "If you see me go to heaven, you shall have your desire."

TALK TIME
Do you know a person who follows and loves God? Would you like to learn from them? Why?

PRAYER TIME
Dear God, please give me good people in my life that love you. Amen.

BIBLE TIME
2 Kings 2: verses 11-15

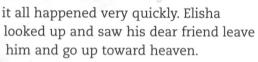

Elijah goes to Heaven

As Elijah and Elisha were walking and talking along the road together, there suddenly appeared a brilliant chariot of fire drawn by horses.

The chariot reached Elijah and took him up to heaven...

it all happened very quickly. Elisha looked up and saw his dear friend leave him and go up toward heaven.

Elisha stood and cried out to Elijah, but the horses and the chariot had disappeared.

Elisha was saddened; he had lost someone who he loved very much.

Gently he picked up Elijah's cloak that had fallen on the ground.

TALK TIME

Do you know of anyone who has died? How might you comfort that person's family?

PRAYER TIME

Dear God, please bring comfort to people who have lost a dear friend or relative. May your love be with them. Amen.

146

BIBLE TIME
2 Kings 2: verses 13-15

Elisha the prophet

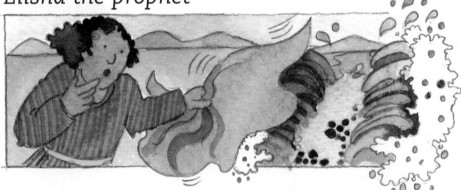

Elisha picked up Elijah's cloak. He was still saddened that Elijah had gone, and he missed him very much. He remembered that Elijah had said that if that he saw him go to up heaven, he too would become a prophet just like him.

Elisha then struck the water of the Jordan River with Elijah's cloak... suddenly the water divided in front of his very eyes...! What a miracle!

Other prophets standing nearby looked on with amazement.

"Now we know," they said, "that Elisha, too, will be a prophet," they said.

TALK TIME
Look back at Day 133 and see who else was amazed when they saw a miracle from God.

PRAYER TIME
Dear God, thank you for your miracles. Thank you for Elijah and Elisha, who both wanted to follow you. Amen.

BIBLE TIME
2 Kings 2: verses 19-23

Bullying and jeering

Some men came up to Elisha and said that their town was a good town... but it had bad water. So Elisha asked them to bring a bowl of water with salt in it. Elisha threw this salty water into the bad water and immediately the water became pure... another miracle from God!

In the next town that Elisha visited he came across a group of young people. They bullied and jeered at Elisha and pointed their fingers at him and said, "Go away, baldhead!"

They shouted and laughed at him.

TALK TIME
Has anyone ever bullied you? Talk about it.

PRAYER TIME
Dear God, please protect all those who have been bullied and jeered at. Please stand by their side and stand up for them. Amen.

BIBLE TIME
2 Kings 4: verses 1-3

Helping a woman

As Elisha was walking along, a woman cried out to him.

"My husband is dead!" she cried. "My children and I are in debt and people are coming to take my two sons away from me!"

Elisha looked at her and tenderly said, "How can I help you? What do you have in your house?"

The woman went back into her house and then came out and told Elisha, "I have only a little oil."

Elisha said to her, "Now go to all your neighbors and ask them to give you empty jars, as many as possible, and then take them into your house."

TALK TIME
Do you know someone who needs help? How can you help?

PRAYER TIME
Dear God, help me to help others who need your help. Amen.

BIBLE TIME
2 Kings 4: verses 4-7

Another miracle!

Elisha then told the woman, "When you have gathered many, many jars, take them into your home. Let your sons be with you." He continued, "Pour a little of the oil into each jar and as each one is filled up with oil, put it aside."

The woman did just as Elisha had told her. Gradually, every jar became full to the brim with oil!

Then everyone knew that this man named Elisha was a man of God. When every jar had been filled with oil, the woman went outside to Elisha.

He said to her, "Now go and sell the oil in the jars, and you will be able to pay off all your debts."

The woman and her two sons were delighted; they knew that they had been helped by God.

TALK TIME
What do you like about this story? How do you think the mother felt?

PRAYER TIME
Dear God, thank you that you helped this poor mother out of debt and that she and her sons could eat again. Amen.

BIBLE TIME
2 Kings 5: verses 1-5

Naaman, a commander

There was a man who belonged to a great army in a foreign country. His name was Naaman. He was an excellent leader and was very brave. His master liked him very much.

But poor Naaman had leprosy.

One day a servant girl, who was from Israel, said, "I know of a prophet from my land who would heal Naaman. His name is Elisha."

When Naaman was told about this, he went to his master of the army and asked for permission to go and see Elisha.

"Go," said the master, "I will also send a letter to the king of Israel to say that you are going to see this man."

TALK TIME
Do you ever write or receive letters or cards? Who would you like to send a card to and when?

PRAYER TIME
Dear God, thank you that this king wanted Naaman to go and see Elisha. Amen.

BIBLE TIME
2 Kings 5: verses 7-8

A message

When the king of Israel received the letter from the master of the army concerning Naaman, he became very angry and said, "Why is this fellow sending this man to be cured here? We can't help him."

Elisha said to the king of Israel, "Let Naaman come, for then he will know that there is a prophet in the land of Israel."

So Naaman eventually arrived at Elisha's house.

Then Elisha sent a messenger out to Naaman saying, "Go and wash yourself in the River Jordan seven times, and you will be healed."

TALK TIME
What do you think Naaman thought when he heard this?

PRAYER TIME
Dear God, sometimes you tell us to do something that we don't understand. Help me to know that you are always in control. Amen.

BIBLE TIME
2 Kings 5: verses 11-12

Naaman gets angry

"Go and wash in the River Jordan!" shouted Naaman. He was angry with the message from Elisha. "Surely he should have come out of his house and come to me. Why didn't he call on his God to heal me from my leprosy!"

Naaman's fury continued. "The rivers back home are just as good as the River Jordan; why didn't this prophet ask me to dip in one of those?"

Naaman turned to go back home. He was very angry and furious.

Naaman's servant ran after him and said, "This prophet has not told you to do something difficult... so why don't you do it?"

TALK TIME
Do you ever get angry? What do you get angry about?

PRAYER TIME
If I have ever been angry or cross, I am so sorry. Dear Lord, please forgive me. Help me not to get angry again. Amen.

BIBLE TIME
2 Kings 5: verses 14-16

He did as he was told

After listening to Elisha's servants
telling him to go to the River Jordan
and dip in it seven times, Naaman did as he was
asked and walked toward the river.

He took his outer garment off and his sandals. Then he very gently
stepped into the river.

He did this seven times just as Elisha had told
him to do.

After the seventh time
Naaman came out of
the River Jordan healed
from leprosy. All of his
skin was very smooth!

He knew then that
there was a powerful
God of Israel!

TALK TIME
Talk about why God does miracles.

PRAYER TIME
*Dear God, it's so great to learn how you do miracles and heal
people. Thank you for healing Naaman. Amen.*

BIBLE TIME
2 Kings 5: verses 15-19

No gifts please

Naaman was thankful that
the God of Israel had healed him.
His skin was now cleared from the
leprosy. He was grateful to Elisha for
telling him to dip into the River
Jordan. He knew that this man was
from God.

"Please, I want to give you a big gift,"
said Naaman to Elisha.

"No," replied Elisha. "As surely I serve
God, I won't accept a thing from you."

"Then," said Naaman, "I will not
worship any other god but your
God. May He forgive me for having
other idols."

Elisha then said to Naaman, "Go in peace."

TALK TIME
*What do you like about Naaman? Does this story teach you
about obeying God?*

PRAYER TIME
*Dear God, I love it when people turn to you in obedience and
you do miracles in their lives! Amen.*

BIBLE TIME

Jeremiah 1: verses 1-14;
Jeremiah 2: verses 29-30

A picture

A young man named Jeremiah lived in the land of Israel. God had chosen him as a prophet and wanted him to warn the people in Israel to turn back and worship Him only.

"But," said Jeremiah to God, "I don't know how to speak to the people... I am far too young and know nothing."

God told him not to be afraid because He was with him. Then God touched Jeremiah's mouth and said, "Now I have put the words in your mouth. What do you see?"

Jeremiah said he saw a boiling pot tilted away from the north.

"The meaning of this picture," said God, "is that my people will turn against me, but you must go and tell them not to do this for I will bring punishment on them."

TALK TIME

Has anyone said that you are far too young to do something? Talk about it.

PRAYER TIME

Dear God, help me to do and say things that are right with you. Amen.

BIBLE TIME

Jeremiah 1: verses 16 and 19;
Jeremiah 25: verse 11

Disaster!

God said to Jeremiah that disaster would come to the land of Israel because the people were turning to other gods.

He told Jeremiah to be strong and to say what was going to happen to His people, even though they would be against him.

God told Jeremiah to go to them and tell them what He was going to do.

"I want my people to turn back to me from their wicked ways," said God.

Then the cities were destroyed, and there was a famine. Many of the people of Israel were led away as prisoners to the land of Babylon.

TALK TIME

Can you remember the names of other prophets of God?
Look at Day 125 and Day 140

PRAYER TIME

Dear God, I am so glad that you prepare us for things to come.
Help me to listen to you when you are trying to tell me something.
Amen.

BIBLE TIME
Daniel 1: verses 1-3

Four young friends

Many of the people of Israel had been captured from their ruined towns and villages, just as God had said through the prophet Jeremiah. They were taken off to a land called Babylon. The people there did not worship the God of Israel but worshipped many different idols and gods.

One day, King Nebuchadnezzar of Babylon ordered his servants to bring him some young men from the captured Israelites. He wanted them to serve him in many ways in the palace. Among the group chosen was a very young man named Daniel and three of his friends, Shadrach, Meshach, and Abednego. The four of them were handsome and very wise.

TALK TIME
Who are your best friends and why? What are their names?

PRAYER TIME
Dear God, thank you so much for giving me friends.
They are very special to me. Amen.

BIBLE TIME
Daniel 1: verses 4-15

Bad food

Now the king of Babylon told his servants to give the very best food and drink to these four young men. They were to be trained for three years, after which they would serve him in his palace.

Daniel didn't like the rich food and wine that the king gave them. He asked if they could have only vegetables to eat and water to drink.

"But that won't do you much good!," exclaimed the king's servant. "You must build up your strength with the king's best food."

However, they were given the food that they asked for, and after ten days Daniel and his friends looked much healthier than any of the others in the palace!

TALK TIME
What's your favorite food and why?

PRAYER TIME
Dear God, thank you for all the food that you give us to eat. Amen.

BIBLE TIME
Daniel 1: verses 17-18

Very clever

God had given to each of these four friends a lot of wisdom and knowledge, and they were quick to learn. They all learned how to speak another language, and they read from many scrolls. They very quickly learned how to live among the Babylonian people.

Now God had given Daniel a very special gift. If someone had a dream or a vision, Daniel could explain the meaning of the dream. Very soon God was going to use Daniel's gift with King Nebuchadnezzar.

 TALK TIME

What do you like to learn? What is your favorite subject at school? Say something that you have learned from a teacher/parent/caregiver recently.

 PRAYER TIME

Dear God, help me to learn a lot. When it becomes too hard for me, I will pray to you so that you can help me. Amen.

Wisdom and knowledge

After three years, Daniel and his friends were presented to King Nebuchadnezzar. They had spent the last three years studying and learning.

"In my palace there is no one as clever," said the king, "as you four young men."

The friends had been trained well. Little did the king know that it was God who had given these four young men SO much wisdom and knowledge.

The king found them all very bright and intelligent!

TALK TIME
Who else had great wisdom? Look at Day 119.

PRAYER TIME
Dear God, thank you for your wisdom. Please may I have this today in all that I do and say. Amen.

BIBLE TIME
Daniel 2: verses 1-16

A bad dream

King Nebuchadnezzar could not sleep because he was having bad dreams. So he called together men who he thought would be able to understand his dreams. They all had magic powers, and the king wanted these men to tell him what his dreams meant.

They all failed to come up with an answer!

"There is not a man on earth who could understand your dreams," said one of the magic men. "What you're asking us to do is far too difficult."

But it wasn't too difficult for one young man... and that was Daniel.

He believed that the God of Israel would help him.

TALK TIME
Go to Day 153 and see why it wasn't too difficult for Daniel!

PRAYER TIME
Dear God, thank you that you gave a gift to Daniel of interpreting dreams, and he was able to know the meaning of the king's dream. Amen.

BIBLE TIME
Daniel 2: verses 16-23

Pray hard!

Daniel knew the magic men couldn't give a meaning to King Nebuchadnezzar's dreams, so he went to the king and asked, "Please will you give me time to interpret your dreams?"

The king agreed.

Daniel went back to his three friends, Shadrach, Meshach, and Abednego, and he urged them to pray about the situation.

During the night Daniel had a vision. God spoke to him about the king's dreams. Daniel praised God and thanked Him for giving him such wisdom.

He went to the king and said, "There is only one God in Heaven who can reveal mysteries, and He has shown me about your dreams."

TALK TIME
When do you pray? Who do you like to pray with?

PRAYER TIME
Dear God, thank you that Daniel's friends prayed for him through the situation. Help me to pray more often to you about hard situations and also for my family and friends. Amen.

BIBLE TIME
Daniel 2: verses 31-35

The meaning of the dream

"In your dream," said Daniel to the king, "you saw a big gold statue towering above you. It was made of gold, bronze, iron, and clay. A stone came and smashed the statue and reduced it to pieces, and the wind blew it all away. But the stone that hit the statue became a huge mountain and filled the whole earth." The king sat in silence as he listened to Daniel.

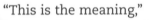

"This is the meaning," continued Daniel. "The statue's head stands for you, O king. The other parts of the statue stand for other countries, some great, others small... but none of them will last. The stone that was thrown at the statue stands for the kingdom of God. For God, who is far greater than anyone on earth, will last forever."

TALK TIME
How is God great and strong?

PRAYER TIME
Dear God, I am so grateful that you are more powerful, stronger, and greater than anything else on this earth. Amen.

BIBLE TIME
Daniel 2: verses 46-49

Honor

King Nebuchadnezzar knew that Daniel's interpretation of his dream was true. He saw that God had shown him what would happen in the future.

Then the king knelt down at Daniel's feet and paid honor to him.

"Surely," he said to Daniel, "your God is the God of all gods, for he was able to give me a meaning to my dream."

After this Daniel was given a very high position in the king's palace. King Nebuchadnezzar made him a ruler in Babylon, placed him in charge of wise men, and gave him many gifts. The king also gave good jobs to Daniel's three friends – Shadrach, Meshach, and Abednego.

TALK TIME
What job would you like when you're older?
Why would you like this job?

PRAYER TIME
Dear God, I look forward to the job that you have planned for me when I'm older. Amen.

BIBLE TIME
Daniel 3: verses 1-3

Giving orders

Some while later, King Nebuchadnezzar gave orders for a huge golden statue to be built in a place called Dura.

Then King Nebuchadnezzar commanded all his officers, governors, captains, and staff to come and worship the statue. He even told them to come to the opening ceremony and worship the statue as a god!

So all the people arrived and bowed down to this gold statue. Trumpets blew, and music played. There was a lot of noise!

Everyone did as the king ordered... except Daniel's three friends Shadrach, Meshach, and Abednego. They all refused to worship a false god.

TALK TIME
Have you ever refused to do something because you felt it wasn't the right thing to do? Talk about it.

PRAYER TIME
Dear God, please tell me when it is wrong to do something. Help me to hear you and obey you. Amen.

BIBLE TIME
Daniel 3: verses 11-18

An angry king!

Some of the group saw that Daniel's three friends didn't fall down and worship the golden statue. This group hurried off to tell the king. "They don't serve your god or fall down at the feet of the golden statue," they reported to the king. King Nebuchadnezzar was angry! "How dare they not obey me?" he shouted. "Go and get them." So Daniel's three friends were brought before the king.

"If you don't worship my statue... I will throw you all into a fiery furnace and burn you to death!" he told them.

"We will not worship your false god," the three friends said. "And our God of Israel will protect us from your fiery furnace."

TALK TIME
Why weren't Shadrach, Meshach, and Abednego afraid?

PRAYER TIME
Dear Lord, thank you for all the ways that you have protected me today. Amen.

BIBLE TIME
Daniel 3: verses 19-23

Ablaze

King Nebuchadnezzar flew into a rage! He was furious that Shadrach, Meshach, and Abednego would not worship his golden statue.

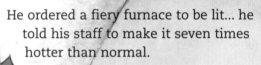

He ordered a fiery furnace to be lit... he told his staff to make it seven times hotter than normal.

Then he told his soldiers to tie up the three friends and throw them into the fire.

The fire was very hot when the three friends were thrown into the furnace.

As King Nebuchadnezzar stood and watched the young men in the fire, he suddenly saw, to his amazement, not three men in the fiery furnace... but four!

TALK TIME
What do you think the king thought?

PRAYER TIME
Dear God, I always love it when you amaze people! Thank you that you did this to King Nebuchadnezzar. Amen.

BIBLE TIME
Daniel 3: verses 24-30

Saved by God

"Didn't we put three men into the fire?" shouted the king. "Now there are four walking around in the furnace!"

The king went to the opening of the fire and yelled into the flames, "Shadrach, Meshach, and Abednego, servants of God, come out!"

The three friends walked out of the fire. Everyone saw that the flames and heat had not burned them at all... their hair and clothes had not been singed; they didn't even smell of fire!

"Praise to your God," said the king. "He sent you an angel to protect you in the fire. You may always worship your God of Israel."

TALK TIME
What do you love about God when He wants people to know who He is?

PRAYER TIME
Dear God of heaven, thank you that you moved in power with King Nebuchnezzar so that he would know who you are. Amen.

BIBLE TIME
Daniel 6: verses 1-5

A new king

King Darius, the next king of Babylon, was so impressed with Daniel's wisdom that he gave him a promotion in the palace.

This made Daniel the most powerful man next to the king.

The other palace officials became jealous and got together and began plotting how they could get rid of Daniel and remove him from his job.

But no one could find fault with Daniel because he was so trustworthy and honest!

"The only way we can get rid of him," they agreed, "is to make him do something against his God."

TALK TIME
Trustworthy means reliable. What ways have you trusted God today?

PRAYER TIME
Dear God, thank you that Daniel was honest and people trusted him. Thank you that I can trust you always. Amen.

BIBLE TIME
Daniel 6: verses 6-10

A new law

The officials went to the king and asked him to make a new law. They said that under the new law everyone should pray to the king and not to any other god.

Everyone would be forced to do this for the next thirty days and anyone found disobeying this law should be thrown into the lions' den.

So the king made it a law for all the people... he liked it that his people would pray only to him!

When Daniel heard about the new law, he went home to pray to God, next to his open window... just like he had done before.

TALK TIME
What have you prayed today? Have you asked for God's help for anything?

PRAYER TIME
Dear God, I am so glad that I can come to you for help. I know you will hear me just as you heard Daniel. Amen.

BIBLE TIME
Daniel 6: verses 11-14

A sad king

The officials could see Daniel praying through his window. They could see that he was kneeling and praying not to the king but to the God of Israel. At last! They had found something that would make Daniel fall from the powerful job that he held in the palace. So they went to the king and reported what they had seen Daniel do.

"That law you made, saying that no one was to pray to anyone else but you. Well... we have to tell you that we saw Daniel praying to his God of Israel. He has disobeyed you, and the law says that he must be thrown into the lions' den!"

King Darius was extremely sad. Daniel was his favorite official.

TALK TIME
What do you think of these officials who reported back to the king?

PRAYER TIME
Dear God, help me never to talk about friends behind their backs. Thank you, Lord, that you help me in all ways. Amen.

BIBLE TIME
Daniel 6: verses 14-16

Trying to save

King Darius was so upset that Daniel was found breaking the law. It was his officials who had suggested this law to him, and he had signed it.

He desperately wanted to rescue Daniel from the lions' den and for many hours made every effort to save him.

"NO!" his officials said. "You signed the law, and now you can't change it."

As Daniel was taken towards the lions' den, the king said to Daniel,

"May the God you serve rescue you."

Then Daniel was thrown into the den and to the waiting hungry lions.

TALK TIME

What do you like about Daniel? Do you think he was very brave?

PRAYER TIME

Dear God, I want to be always brave, faithful, honest, and trustworthy just like Daniel. Amen.

BIBLE TIME
Daniel 6: verses 17-23

Protected

A very large stone was placed over the lions' den. It left Daniel alone and in the dark with several big lions, who snarled and roared in a very hungry way! The king thought about Daniel all night long. He couldn't eat or sleep because he was so worried. He hoped that Daniel's God would protect him from the lions.

Early next morning the king rushed to the den. "Daniel, Daniel," he cried, "has your God protected you?"

Daniel's voice could be heard deep from within the den, "I am here... my God sent an angel, and he shut the mouths of the lions." The king was overjoyed! He then had Daniel taken out from the den and saw that the lions had not even scratched him.

TALK TIME
What noise does a lion make?

PRAYER TIME
Dear God of heaven, thank you that you looked after Daniel and protected him from the roaring hungry lions. Amen.

BIBLE TIME
Nehemiah 1: verses 1-4

Forgiveness

Many of the Israelite people were captured as prisoners from Israel. One of them was Nehemiah.

Nehemiah was a cupbearer in a far off country. That meant he had to taste the king's drinks to make sure no poison had been put into them.

One day Nehemiah heard about Jerusalem and how the enemy had destroyed the city.

He cried for days and prayed to God. He also asked for forgiveness from God because his people had been disobedient.

"You have promised," prayed Nehemiah to God, "that if we keep your commands, you will bring us back to live in the land of Israel. Forgive us, O Lord, for not keeping your laws."

TALK TIME
Is there anything today that you should ask God's forgiveness for?

PRAYER TIME
Dear God, if I have not been as good as I should today, please forgive me. Amen.

BIBLE TIME
Nehemiah 2: verses 2-5

Sad heart

One day Nehemiah took a drink to the king.
After testing it, Nehemiah handed it to the king.

Nehemiah felt sad. "Why are you looking so sad?" asked the king.

"The city I used to live in," replied Nehemiah, "is in ruins. Jerusalem was the home of all my family, but now it has all been destroyed."

"What would you like?" asked the king.

Nehemiah prayed quietly and then said, "I long to return to Jerusalem to rebuild it."

So the king granted Nehemiah his desire and even supplied the wood to help him rebuild the city of Jerusalem.

TALK TIME
Have you ever felt sad for one of your friends?
Can you say why?

PRAYER TIME
Dear God, please help me to understand when one of my friends is sad. Help me to be a good friend to them. Amen.

BIBLE TIME
Nehemiah 2: verses 11-19

Rebuilding

It was nighttime when Nehemiah set off. He rode through the dark with a few men.

Eventually they came to Jerusalem and began to examine the city walls. The walls had all been burnt down and destroyed.

"Come," said Nehemiah, "let's start to build the walls again. I know the hand of God is upon us... so let's get started!"

So Nehemiah and his workmen began to rebuild. However, nearby there was a group of people who mocked Nehemiah and his helpers.

TALK TIME
To mock is to make fun of. Has there ever been a time when someone has done this to you? How did you feel?

PRAYER TIME
Dear God, help me to forgive people who make fun of others or me. Amen.

BIBLE TIME
Nehemiah 3: verses 1-32

Gates and walls

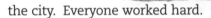

Everyone worked in groups to rebuild Jerusalem. They repaired gates around the city walls. Each gate had a name like sheep gate, fish gate, old gate, and fountain gate.

The workers gathered rocks and bricks, wood and stones... bolts were put back onto the doors of each gate. Steps were built back up again. Hammering could be heard all over the city. Everyone worked hard.

Jerusalem was being repaired, and everyone was happy.

Well, nearly everyone. There were some enemies who didn't like what Nehemiah and his helpers were doing. They even wanted to attack them.

TALK TIME
Do you help doing jobs around the house?
What do you enjoy doing?

PRAYER TIME
Dear God, help me to do jobs in my home... like picking up my room. Amen.

BIBLE TIME

BIBLE TIME
Nehemiah 4: verses 11-23

Keep going

Nehemiah saw that his workers were afraid of the enemies who were very close to the city of Jerusalem.

"Don't be afraid! Remember, God is awesome!"

Nehemiah instructed the workers to carry swords with them, so they could defend themselves if the enemy attacked. He also told everyone that if they heard a trumpet, they should all run to the spot and protect the person who was in trouble.

The plan worked well and the rebuilding continued.

TALK TIME
Have you had a good plan? Did it work?

PRAYER TIME
Dear Lord, thank you that you were with Nehemiah and the workers. Thank you, too, that your plans always work. Amen.

BIBLE TIME
Nehemiah 5: verses 1-13

Pay the poor

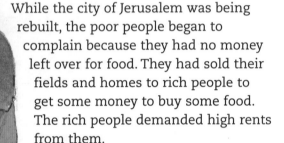

While the city of Jerusalem was being rebuilt, the poor people began to complain because they had no money left over for food. They had sold their fields and homes to rich people to get some money to buy some food. The rich people demanded high rents from them.

So Nehemiah called a large meeting. He told the rich people, "It's not right, what you are doing. The poor will never be able to pay you. Give them back their fields and homes and stop taking money from them." The rich people immediately said to Nehemiah, "We will give it all back and do as you say."

Then all of the rich people promised they would do this and everyone said, "Amen," and praised the Lord.

TALK TIME
Why is it good to give money to the poor?

PRAYER TIME
Dear Lord, thank you that I can give some money to the poor to help them. Amen.

BIBLE TIME
Nehemiah 12: verses 27-47

A celebration!

Hooray, the workers finished rebuilding the walls in fifty-two days! Jerusalem was safe again.

When all the work had been completed, Nehemiah knew that his people needed to turn back to God and follow His rules. They had all been living in other lands and had forgotten God's laws. They wept and asked for God's forgiveness.

Then Nehemiah celebrated the rebuilding of Jerusalem – it was wonderful – choirs, trumpets, dancing!

TALK TIME
What are the ways you celebrate in your church?

PRAYER TIME
Dear God, I am so glad that I am part of your family and can celebrate and praise you all the time. Amen.

BIBLE TIME
Jonah 1: verses 1-3

Go!

The people of Nineveh were very wicked because they had turned their backs on God.

One day God spoke to Jonah, a prophet living in Israel, "Go to the great city of Nineveh and tell them not to be so wicked."

But do you know what Jonah did? Because he didn't want to go and speak to the wicked people, he tried to run away from God. He found a ship and hopped on it. The boat was heading for a place called Tarshish, which was in the completely opposite direction to Nineveh!

Once on board the ship Jonah settled down for the long, long journey.

TALK TIME
What do you think about Jonah going in the opposite direction?

PRAYER TIME
Dear God, please forgive me when I have gone against your will. Help me to always do as you ask. Amen.

BIBLE TIME
Jonah 1: verses 4-9

The Lord's storm

As soon as the ship started to sail, the Lord God sent a storm. It blew and blew. The waves were VERY high. The ship was tossing on the sea, and all the crew on board were terrified.

The captain of the ship went to Jonah who was asleep.

"Wake up!" he shouted to Jonah. "Pray to your God to save us!"

Meanwhile, the crew of the ship pointed their fingers at Jonah – saying it was his fault that they were in such trouble at sea with the storm!

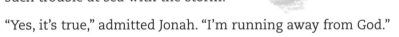

"Yes, it's true," admitted Jonah. "I'm running away from God."

TALK TIME
How do you think God felt about Jonah?

PRAYER TIME
Dear God, there are things that I wish I didn't have to do.
Please help me to do what you want, not what I want. Amen.

BIBLE TIME
Jonah 1: verses 12-17

Overboard

The sea was getting rougher and rougher, and the crew of the ship were getting more and more frightened.

Then Jonah admitted, "This is all my fault. If you throw me overboard, I know the sea will become calm for you."

The men didn't want to do this. They tried to row ashore... but the stormy sea stopped them. Eventually, they decided to throw Jonah overboard... SPLASH! and into the waves he dived.

At once the sea became calm, the wind dropped, and the boat sailed off with the crew.

Jonah began to sink to the bottom of the sea... but then God sent a great big fish that swallowed poor Jonah up whole!

TALK TIME
Have you ever admitted that something was your fault? What happened?

PRAYER TIME
Dear God, please help me to be honest and tell the truth at all times. Amen.

BIBLE TIME
Jonah 2, verses 1-10

A quick prayer...

It wasn't very nice being in the stomach of a very large fish...! Jonah began to pray.

"Help me, God," he prayed. "You have thrown me into the deep waters, and I was drowning. I remember you, O Lord, and am turning to you now. Please save me. I will do anything you ask! Only you can save me."

Poor Jonah was in great distress.

God heard his prayer and told the fish to spit Jonah out. The next thing Jonah knew, he was being hurled from the big fish's mouth onto dry land!

TALK TIME
Why do you think God allowed Jonah to come out of the big fish?

PRAYER TIME
Dear God, thank you for that very special plan for Jonah. Thank you that you told the big fish to spit him out! Amen.

BIBLE TIME
Jonah 3: verses 1-10

Second chance

Then God spoke to Jonah again.

"Go to the city of Nineveh and give them the message I gave to you."

This time Jonah obeyed God. He set off on the long journey to Nineveh. When he arrived there, he walked through it for three days, shouting that God would destroy the city in forty days if they didn't repent of their wickedness.

The king of Nineveh and all the people listened. They believed what Jonah was saying. The king prayed, "We must give up our evil ways and repent. We must change our ways."

He begged God to forgive them. When God saw how sorry they all were, He forgave them and didn't destroy their city.

TALK TIME
Has there ever been a time when you have had to change your ways? What happened?

PRAYER TIME
Dear Lord, thank you that you have so much love for me that you always want me turn to you and say sorry when I have done wrong. Amen.

BIBLE TIME

**Isaiah 7: verse 14;
Isaiah 9: verse 6**

Other prophets

The people of Israel always knew that one day God was going to send them a very special person called the Messiah who would rescue and save them.

God spoke through people called prophets. They told the people what would happen in the future. One of them was named Isaiah. One time he told the people of Israel, "The Lord will give you a sign who that special person will be." He continued, "For some day in the future a very young girl will give birth to a son and one of his names will be 'Immanuel' which means 'God is with us.' He will also be called the Prince of Peace."

TALK TIME

Messiah means "the promised one." Let someone read today's verses from the Bible to you.

PRAYER TIME

Dear God, thank you that you knew all along the plan for the whole world... that you would send your son Jesus the Messiah. Amen.

BIBLE TIME
Isaiah 40: verse 11

Like a shepherd

Isaiah also told the people of Israel that this special person called the Messiah would be like a shepherd to them, and they will be like a flock of sheep. He would lead them, care for them, and guide them.

The Messiah will bring good news to them, and they will want to rejoice. He told them not to be afraid... The Messiah will carry them like lambs in His arms, and they will be close to His heart.

The Messiah wants them to know who He is, for He will walk with them.

TALK TIME
What do you like about sheep? Draw a picture of one.

PRAYER TIME
Dear God, I'm so glad that so many, many years ago you promised your people a Messiah who would be like a shepherd. Amen.

BIBLE TIME
Isaiah 53: verses 1-6

Gone astray

God also told Isaiah that all of His people had gone astray and that they had turned their backs on Him. Isaiah also said, "You will have difficulty in believing who this special person will be, for people will be against Him. He will be

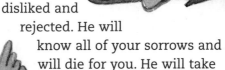

disliked and rejected. He will know all of your sorrows and will die for you. He will take all the wrong that you have done and in return He will forgive you."

Isaiah also told them that they were to sing for joy because this special person would give them a new life.

TALK TIME
Who do think was this special person Isaiah talked about all those years ago?

PRAYER TIME
Dear God, thank you that you knew all along the plan for the whole world. Thank you for sending your son Jesus to die for us so that we may know your forgiveness. Amen.

BIBLE TIME

**Micah 3: verse 12;
Micah 5: verses 2 and 5**

In Bethlehem

God sent another prophet named Micah to the people of Israel. He told them that a disaster would come upon them because they believed in false prophets. God was angry with them.

"Walk with love and let God teach you," said Micah.

"Many bad things will happen to you in the land of Israel," he warned them. "But there will come a special person for you," continued Micah. "You will know who this person is for He will be born in a little town called Bethlehem. He will be your shepherd and give you security."

Micah also said that this special person would bring them peace.

TALK TIME

Security means safety. How do you feel secure with God? Explain what peace is.

PRAYER TIME

Dear God, thank you that you give us security and peace when we know about your love. Help me sometimes when I don't have peace. Amen.

BIBLE TIME
Zechariah 9: verse 9

The coming Messiah

There was another prophet that God sent to his people named Zechariah. God wanted His people to know about this special person called the Messiah.

"Rejoice," said Zechariah the prophet. "Shout and sing, you people of Israel! Some day in the future you will see your King coming to you. He will be godly and will save you."

Then Zechariah said that they would know the Messiah because He would ride on a donkey. He would bring peace, and He would rule over the whole world!

TALK TIME
Can you remember what the name Messiah means?
Look at Day 181.

PRAYER TIME
Dear Lord God, I am so glad that you promised us your son, the Messiah, and that He would rule over the whole earth. Amen.

NEW TESTAMENT

Contents

	Page		Page
Zechariah & Elizabeth	194-198	Lepers get well	261-263
Mary and the angel	199-201	A lame man walks	264-268
Joseph	202-203	A blind man sees	269-271
Mary and Elizabeth	204-205	A son is healed	272-274
John	206-207	Friend Lazarus	275-282
Jesus is born	208-210	A huge picnic	283-288
The shepherds hear	211-213	The taxman	289-296
The wise men	214-217	A sheep story	297-301
Giving thanks	218-220	The big party	302-308
Young Jesus	221-224	Good and not good	309-311
Jesus baptized	225-226	Heaven is like	312
The fishermen	227-230	A son leaves home	313-316
First miracle	231-234	A son returns	317-321
A storm	235-238	A kind man	322-327
Martha and Mary	239-242	The sower	328-332
The greatest	243-244	Jesus walks on water	333-338
Jesus loves children	245-246	Jesus heals again	339
Prayer	247-249	Jesus in Jerusalem	340-343
Jesus teaches	250-253	His last meal	344-347
Jesus heals	254-256	Jesus is arrested	348-352
A little girl is healed	257-260	A sad time	353-355
		Jesus is alive!	356-365
		The Holy Spirit comes	366-370
		Tell everyone!	371-373
		Jesus is coming back!	374

The New Testament
Introduction

The prophets had promised
that one day God was going to send the Israelites
someone who would set them free and save
them from hardship.
The prophets also promised that this person
was going to be their Messiah and King.
They waited and waited for Him...

Many years later God did send someone.
This person was very special. He brought
a new message to the world.

His name is Jesus...

BIBLE TIME
Luke 1: verses 5-13

No children

There was a priest named Zechariah who was married to Elizabeth. Both of them obeyed God and all of His commandments and laws.

They were very sad because they didn't have any children. Now they were both quite old.

One evening Zechariah was in the temple going about his duties.

Suddenly an angel named Gabriel appeared. Zechariah became full of fear. Then the Angel Gabriel said to him, "Don't be afraid, Zechariah. The Lord has heard your prayers. I have come to tell you that you and your wife Elizabeth will have a child, and you are to name him John."

TALK TIME
Talk about a time when the Lord has heard your prayers. How did He answer?

PRAYER TIME
Dear God, thank you for all the times that you have heard my prayers and answered them. Amen.

BIBLE TIME
Luke 1: verses 14-16

Such a joy!

Zechariah listened to the Angel Gabriel speaking to him in the temple. The angel told him that he and his wife, Elizabeth, were going to have a baby.

"Your child," the Angel Gabriel said, "will be such a joy and delight to you. Many people will be happy because of his birth. He will be great in the sight of the Lord, and he will point the way to God. Many people will return to God, praising Him.

The angel also told Zechariah that the baby's name would be John, and that he would be full of the Holy Spirit and prepare people's hearts to meet Jesus when He arrived.

TALK TIME
Do you point the way to God to your friends?
How you do it?

PRAYER TIME
Dear God, thank you that you are my Father in Heaven and that you love me SO much. Amen.

BIBLE TIME
Luke 2: verses 18-20

How will it happen?

Zechariah was a bit puzzled and asked the Angel Gabriel, "How can I be sure of what you are saying? My wife and I are too old to have a child. Surely it is now impossible for us to have one."

The Angel Gabriel answered Zechariah, "I am an angel that stands in the presence of God! He has sent me to speak to you and give you this good news. But now you have not believed my words. Because of this, as from today, you will not be able to speak. Only when the baby is born will you be able to speak."

TALK TIME
How did Zechariah feel when the Angel Gabriel told him what would happen? Talk about some of the things you believe in.

PRAYER TIME
Dear heavenly Father, thank you that you were with Zechariah, even though he didn't believe the angel and wouldn't be able to speak until the baby arrived. Amen.

BIBLE TIME
Luke 2: verses 21-23

Speechless

While the Angel Gabriel had been talking to Zechariah inside the temple, a large crowd had gathered outside waiting for him. Everyone wondered why he was taking so long seeing to his duties. At last Zechariah came out of the temple, but... guess what? Just as the angel had said, he wasn't able to say a word to the crowd. He was speechless.

He couldn't explain to the crowd what that the angel had said to him. So Zechariah had to remain silent about the news of him and his wife having a baby. Poor Zechariah!

TALK TIME
Pretend that you are Zechariah. How would you explain to the crowd what had happened in the temple? Remember you're not allowed to use any words!

PRAYER TIME
Dear God, please help all those who find it difficult to speak – just like Zechariah. Amen.

BIBLE TIME
Luke 1: verses 23-25

A baby!

When Zechariah's time was up doing his duties in the temple, he returned home to Elizabeth his wife.

A little while later, Elizabeth became pregnant. They were both delighted and full of joy!

Elizabeth had to take it easy though, and she stayed indoors for five months.

Elizabeth praised the Lord saying, "The Lord has given me such a big blessing. Both Zechariah and I are old, but the Lord has shown His care and given us a child... even though we're old. Praise His name!"

TALK TIME
Can you talk about a big blessing you've had recently from the Lord?

PRAYER TIME
Dear God, thank you for the blessing you gave Zechariah and Elizabeth. Thank you for all the blessings you give us, too. Amen.

BIBLE TIME
Luke 1: verses 26-33

Chosen by God

Some time later, the Lord sent an angel named Gabriel to Nazareth. He had a special message for a young girl who lived there... her name was Mary.

"Greetings to you," said the Angel Gabriel to her. "You have found favor in the eyes of the Lord, and He is with you."

Mary was very puzzled and surprised by the angel's words. The Angel Gabriel spoke again. "Don't be afraid, Mary, the Lord is happy with you. He has chosen you to give birth to a baby boy. You're to give Him the name of Jesus. He will be the son of the Most High, and His kingdom will go on for ever and ever."

TALK TIME
Look at Day 180 in the Old Testament. See which prophet said that this would happen.

PRAYER TIME
Dear God, thank you that all along you knew that you were going to send your son Jesus to us. Amen.

BIBLE TIME
Luke 1: verses 34-37

Everything is possible!

"Me!" said Mary, "Give birth to a baby? But I'm not married. How will all of this happen?"

The Angel Gabriel replied, "The Holy Spirit will come upon you, and God's power will be with you. The baby you have will be the Son of God."

The Angel Gabriel then told Mary that her cousin Elizabeth and her husband Zechariah were also going to have a boy. This was also a miracle from heaven, as Elizabeth was very old!

"Everything is possible with God!" continued the angel to Mary.

TALK TIME
God had a very special plan for Mary. What plans does the Lord have for you today?

PRAYER TIME
Dear Father God, help me to say "Yes" to the plans you have for me today and to follow them. Amen.

BIBLE TIME
Luke 1: verse 38

So blessed

Mary listened to the Angel Gabriel speaking to her. She felt so blessed that God had chosen her to give birth to His Son. Mary knew that all the Jewish people were expecting someone special to be with them. Now God was asking her to be the mother of this very special baby.

She knew that He would grow up to be great and do many wonderful things among His people.

"I am God's servant," said Mary to the Angel Gabriel, " I am willing to serve God, for I know all this will happen just as you have told me."

Then the Angel Gabriel left her.

TALK TIME
A servant means somebody who helps. What are some ways we can serve the Lord?

PRAYER TIME
Dear God, help me to help other people every day. I want to be a servant for you always. Amen.

BIBLE TIME
Matthew 1: verses 18-25

Joseph is told

Mary was engaged to be married to
Joseph, who was a very good man. But
when he found out that Mary was going
to have a baby, he thought the best thing to do was to leave her.

One night after Joseph fell asleep, an angel appeared to him and
said, "Don't be afraid, Joseph. The baby that Mary is carrying is from
God's Holy Spirit. The baby is very special because He
will save and forgive people from all the wrongs they
have done. So," the angel continued, "go and take
Mary as your wife. When the baby is born, you are to
give Him the name of
Jesus."

TALK TIME
Why is Jesus so special?

PRAYER TIME
*Dear Lord, thank you that you gave us baby Jesus, because He is
so special to me. Amen.*

BIBLE TIME
Matthew 2: verses 21-25

Joseph marries Mary

The angel went on to tell Joseph more things in the dream. He told Joseph of the words that the prophet said many years ago.

"Mary will give birth to a son. His name will also be 'Immanuel', which means 'God with us'. The baby Mary is expecting will be a very special child."

Everything was happening just as God had promised through the prophet.

A little while later, Joseph woke up. He knew that God had spoken to him through the angel.

He then went to Mary and married her.

TALK TIME
Look at Day 180 and see the name of the prophet who said these words.

PRAYER TIME
Dear God, I'm so glad you know the beginning and the end of everything. I feel safe with you. Amen.

BIBLE TIME
Luke 1: verses 39-45

Relatives

Mary wanted to tell her cousin Elizabeth all that had happened to her. So she left her house and walked to Elizabeth's village in the hills.

Elizabeth saw Mary coming and went out to greet her. Something wonderful happened. The baby growing inside Elizabeth's tummy jumped for joy!

"How happy I feel," said Elizabeth to Mary, "that the Lord should send you here. I know the baby that you're carrying is very special, and you will be so blessed."

Elizabeth was filled with joy from the Lord!

TALK TIME
Talk about the joy the Lord gives you.

PRAYER TIME
Dear Heavenly Father, the Bible says that you knew me even when I was a baby inside my mommy's tummy. Thank you for creating me and for the joy you give me daily. Amen.

BIBLE TIME
Luke 1: verses 46-55

Singing a song

Mary was so overjoyed that God had chosen her to be the mother of Jesus that she sang a song to the Lord.

"I bring glory to the Lord for He is my Savior. He has done great things for me. He is holy, and we should fear Him. He has saved the humble and helped the poor. He will always keep His promises to us. Praise Him."

Mary stayed with Elizabeth for three months and then she returned to her home in Nazareth and her new husband Joseph.

TALK TIME
Sing a song that praises the Lord.

PRAYER TIME
Dear God, I think you are wonderful and marvelous. Thank you for all the things you have done for me. Amen.

BIBLE TIME
Luke 1: verses 57-66

Zechariah speaks

Not long after Mary left her house and returned to Nazareth, Elizabeth gave birth to a baby boy. All her neighbors and friends were very happy for her and her husband Zechariah. The Lord had given them a child in their old age!

Elizabeth told everyone, "His name is John."

Even Zechariah, Elizabeth's husband, agreed on this name. Because he couldn't speak, he wrote the name "JOHN" on a tablet of stone.

As soon as he did this, Zechariah could speak. What a miracle!

Everyone praised God. They knew that there was something special about this baby John.

TALK TIME
Have you ever seen a miracle or heard about one?
Talk about it.

PRAYER TIME
Dear God, thank you for all the miracles that you perform.
Thank you for healing Zechariah, and thank you for baby John.
Amen.

BIBLE TIME

Luke 1: verse 80;
Mark 1: verses 1-8

Preparing the way

John grew up to be a healthy young man. He became very strong, believed in the Lord, and walked very closely to Him.

John knew that one day he would meet a very special person. He knew that he had to prepare people's hearts to meet Him. He also knew he would baptize this special person... one day...

John looked and waited for this special person. He knew it was going to be Jesus.

TALK TIME

Has there been a time when you have waited for the Lord to do something in your life?

PRAYER TIME

Dear heavenly Father, when I want you to do something, I pray you would help me to understand that you have perfect timing. Amen.

BIBLE TIME
Luke 2: verses 1-5

A long journey

Now there was a ruler in Israel named Caesar Augustus. He wanted to take a census and count how many people lived in the country. So he ordered all the people to return to the place where they were born.

So Joseph and Mary got ready to leave Nazareth and return to Bethlehem. They packed up all their belongings and saddled up their donkey. It was going to be a long, long journey for them.

Joseph put Mary on the donkey because she was pregnant and found it really hard to walk, as the baby was growing bigger inside her.

They set off to walk the many miles back to Bethlehem. It would take a long time.

TALK TIME
Do you enjoy walking? What do you like about it?

PRAYER TIME
Dear heavenly Father, it's comforting to know that you walk with us daily. Thank you. Amen.

BIBLE TIME
Luke 2: verses 6-7

No room

After many days of journeying, Joseph and Mary arrived in Bethlehem. They were both very weary and tired from traveling such a long distance.

Joseph began to search and search for a room where they could stay the night. Mary followed her husband on the donkey as he knocked on several doors asking for a room to sleep in for the night.

Every hotel they went to was full... there simply wasn't anywhere for them to stay!

Finally, a hotelkeeper let them sleep in the only space left... it was a stable.

Mary and Joseph were just so relieved they had a place to sleep for the night.

TALK TIME
Have you ever visited a stable? What do you think they are like?

PRAYER TIME
Dear God, thank you that you found a place for Mary and Joseph to lie down for the night when they were so tired. Amen.

BIBLE TIME
Luke 2: verse 6

The special baby!

All the animals gathered around Joseph and Mary as they settled in for the night. There were sheep, cattle, a donkey, and birds. They all gazed at the two people who had joined them in the stable.

During the night Mary gave birth to a baby boy. She gently wrapped him up in a cloth and placed him in the manger.

They called the baby Jesus.

Mary and Joseph both knew that they had been chosen by God, and the baby born during the night was a very special child... not only to them, but to the whole world. How special!

TALK TIME
What do you love about Jesus?

PRAYER TIME
Dear Father God, thank you for Joseph and Mary. Help me to have room in my heart for Jesus. Amen.

BIBLE TIME
Luke 2: verses 8-9

Shepherds in a field

The night Jesus was born there were some shepherds not very far away. They were watching over their sheep and keeping them safe in a field.

God sent an angel to talk to the shepherds. The sky lit up and the glory of the Lord shone all around them. The light was SO brilliant!

When the shepherds saw the light, they shook with fright!

But an angel said to them, "Don't be afraid, we bring you some good news."

TALK TIME

Do you remember another time an angel appeared to someone and told them not to be afraid? Look at Days 190 and 193.

PRAYER TIME

Dear Heavenly Father, I like it when you want to do something, and you tell people not to be afraid. Help me never to be afraid, because you are near me. Amen.

BIBLE TIME
Luke 2: verses 11–14

Good news

The angels gathered all around the shepherds on the hillside and an angel said to them, "Today a baby was born in Bethlehem. His name is Jesus. He is Christ the Lord. Go and look for him. You will find Him lying in a manger."

The angel was joined by hundreds more who filled the sky. They were all praising God, saying, "Glory to God in the highest!"

They sang and sang, and, after a short while, the angels returned to Heaven.

The shepherds knew that something very special had happened, so they hurried off to find the baby the angels had spoken about.

TALK TIME
What would you have thought if you had been a shepherd on those hills?

PRAYER TIME
Dear God, it is so wonderful to know about your glory. I want to sing and praise you all day long. Amen.

BIBLE TIME
Luke 2: verses 16-20

Spreading the word...

At last, the shepherds found the stable where they knew they would find the special baby.

When they went inside and saw baby Jesus, they immediately knelt down at the manger.

They knew this baby was the Messiah who they had been looking forward to for such a long time. They also knew that He was the person from God who would save them all and bring them into His kingdom.

The shepherds ran and told the people in Bethlehem what the angels had told them and how they found Jesus... their Messiah.

TALK TIME
Can you remember what Messiah means? Look at Talk Time on Day 180.

PRAYER TIME
Dear God, help me to tell other people about Jesus and how He is so amazing. Thank you that you promised Him to us. Amen.

BIBLE TIME
Matthew 2: verses 1-2

A star

In a far off country some wise men had been following a very bright star in the sky. They knew that this special star meant a special baby had been born. They also knew that He was to be King of the Jews.

They packed their bags on camels and started to ride out to find this new king.

After a long journey they arrived in Jerusalem and asked, "We have seen the star and have come to look for the new king. Can you tell us were we can find Him?"

TALK TIME
When you find Jesus, you want to worship Him. How do you do this?

PRAYER TIME
Dear Jesus, I'm so glad that I have found you. Thank you for everything that you have done; I want to worship you and to love you. Amen.

BIBLE TIME
Matthew 2: verses 3-6

O little town of Bethlehem

Now the king who ruled in Israel at that time was King Herod. When he heard about the new king being born, he was very upset.

So he called the chief priests and the teachers of the law together and asked them, "Where has this new king been born?"

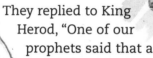

They replied to King Herod, "One of our prophets said that a king would be born in Bethlehem and that he would be a shepherd of Israel."

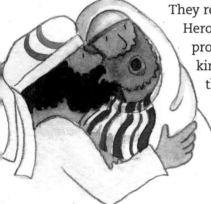

King Herod didn't like the sound of this. Surely, HE was King of Israel!

TALK TIME
Look at Day 183 in the Old Testament and find out the name of the prophet who said that Jesus would be born in Bethlehem.

PRAYER TIME
Dear King Jesus, I'm so glad that you were born and you want to gather us up and love us... just like a shepherd with sheep! Amen.

BIBLE TIME
Matthew 2: verses 7-13

Following the star

After hearing that a new king had been born, King Herod wanted the wise men to call on him. When they arrived, he asked them, "When did this star appear?" The wise men told him.

"Well," said King Herod, "go and search for this new king. As soon as you find him, come back to me so that I may go and worship him."

But really, King Herod wanted to kill the new king... not worship him!

The wise men left the palace, looked up at the sky and saw the star and continued to follow it.

The star went ahead of them until it stopped over a stable in Bethlehem.

TALK TIME
Are you like the wise men... looking for Jesus? How have you found Jesus in your home, school, playtime, and friends?

PRAYER TIME
Dear Jesus, in everything I do today, may I find you. Amen.

BIBLE TIME
Matthew 2: verses 10-11

Gifts for Jesus

At last, after all of their traveling, the wise men were happy when they saw the star stop over a stable.

They went into the stable and found Mary and Joseph with baby Jesus. They walked toward Jesus and bowed down and worshipped Him.

Each of the wise men had brought gifts for Jesus. They presented Him with gold, frankincense, and myrrh. All the wise men knew that in the days to come Jesus would become a very special person and a king.

Just before they were about to leave Bethlehem, the Lord warned them in a dream not to tell King Herod where baby Jesus was, so they returned to their countries taking another route.

TALK TIME
What's the most precious gift you could give Jesus?

PRAYER TIME
Dear Jesus, help me each day give you myself and my love so that you may guide me throughout the day. Amen.

BIBLE TIME
Luke 2: verses 21-24

Presenting Jesus

Mary and Joseph wanted to follow God's laws about babies. That meant they needed to take Him to the temple and present Him to the priest. They also wanted to give thanks to God for giving them Jesus. This was done by offering two doves to God in the temple.

So they set off with Jesus and made their way from Bethlehem to the temple in Jerusalem.

When Joseph, Mary, and Jesus arrived in Jerusalem they entered the temple and found the priest.

TALK TIME
Have you ever thanked God for your life or the lives of people you know? Whose lives would you like to thank the Lord for?

PRAYER TIME
Dear God, thank you that you gave me life and thank you for the lives of.................... Amen.

BIBLE TIME
Luke 2: verses 25-28

Simeon

There lived in Jerusalem a man called Simeon. He loved and followed God.

One day the Holy Spirit told Simeon to go to the temple. So Simeon obeyed and set off. God had promised him that he would see the Messiah before he died... could this be the day, he wondered with excitement!

As Simeon arrived at the temple, he saw Mary and Joseph with baby Jesus. As soon as he saw Jesus he knew immediately that this young child was the promised Messiah from God.

He took Jesus in his arms and praised God saying, "I may now go in peace because my eyes have seen the Messiah who will save Israel and the world."

TALK TIME
What happens when you go to church? Are you excited when you go? Why?

PRAYER TIME
Dear Jesus, please help all people to see who you are, just like Simeon did. Amen.

BIBLE TIME
Luke 2: verses 36-38

Anna

Joseph, Mary, and Jesus were all together in the temple with Simeon, praising God.

Also in the temple that day was a very old woman. Her name was Anna, and she was a prophetess. She never left the temple and praised, worshipped, and prayed to God every day. Sometimes she went without food to pray even harder.

She looked across the temple to where Simeon was holding baby Jesus in his arms. She went over to them and said, "Thank you, God, for this child... the one we have been waiting for. He will save us."

TALK TIME
If you had been there that day, what would you have said to Jesus?

PRAYER TIME
Dear Jesus, I'm so happy that these two saw immediately who you were. Help other people to know you too. Amen.

BIBLE TIME
Luke 2: verses 41-43

A celebration

Joseph, Mary, and Jesus moved to Nazareth. Jesus grew up to be very strong and wise. Each year, they went to a special celebration in Jerusalem called the Feast of the Passover. The people celebrated it to thank God for bringing them out of slavery in Egypt and into the land of Israel and freedom!

Joseph, Mary, and Jesus arrived at the temple in Jerusalem to join in the celebrations. There was singing and praying in the temple, and everyone gathered together to eat and remember that special time.

TALK TIME
Talk about ways you like to celebrate special occasions during the year.

PRAYER TIME
Dear Jesus, thank you that I can celebrate your birthday – a time when we can sing, pray, and thank our Heavenly Father God for you. Amen.

BIBLE TIME
Luke 2: verses 43-44

Lost

After the Feast of Passover was over in Jerusalem, Joseph and Mary packed up to return home to Nazareth along with their friends and relatives.

They thought that Jesus was in the crowd with them. Slowly they made their way along the road home with the crowd, chatting to the friends and relatives as they went.

Suddenly Mary and Joseph realized that Jesus was not with them. He was lost! Mary began to panic.

Jesus was nowhere to be seen.

TALK TIME
Have you heard about a time when someone you know got lost? What happened?

PRAYER TIME
Dear heavenly Father, thank you that we are never lost in your sight. Please help those who have lost someone, and bring that person back. Amen.

BIBLE TIME
Luke 2: verse 45

Back to Jerusalem

Mary and Joseph began to get frantic with worry. Jesus was lost and was nowhere to be seen.

"Have you seen our son?" they asked everyone. "Where can He be?"

"Jesus!" called out Mary. "Jesus, where are you?" But there was no reply.

They looked and searched among the crowds but couldn't find Him. By now Joseph and Mary were very worried.

"Let's go back to Jerusalem," suggested Joseph.

So they both ran as fast as they could back to Jerusalem...
perhaps, they thought, He would still be there.

"Quick," yelled Joseph to Mary, "we must find Him."

TALK TIME
If you were out with your mommy, daddy, or caregiver, and you happened to get lost, what would you do or say?

PRAYER TIME
Dear Heavenly Father, I pray that you will always give me wisdom and help me never to get lost. I pray also that you will always protect me. Amen.

BIBLE TIME
Luke 2: verses 46-48

Found at last!

For three days Joseph and Mary searched for Jesus in Jerusalem. They walked through the streets of the city, searching for Him. They asked many people if they had seen Him. By now they were really worried.

Eventually, on the third day, they found Him!

Jesus was sitting in the temple among the teachers. He was listening to them and asking questions. Everyone there was amazed at His wisdom. But Mary and Joseph were cross with Him. "We've been looking everywhere for you! We were so worried."

But Jesus replied calmly, "Didn't you know I must be in my Father's house?"

TALK TIME
Can you talk about the importance of going to church?

PRAYER TIME
Dear Jesus, I always want to be in your church, learning about you, worshipping you, praying and singing to you. Amen.

BIBLE TIME
Matthew 3: verses 1-4

Saying sorry

As Jesus grew up, his cousin, Elizabeth and Zechariah's son, John, also grew up. He became known as John the Baptist because he prepared people's hearts, told them about Jesus and baptized them.

John dressed in rough woven camel hair clothes with a belt around his waist. He lived in the desert and ate only locusts and honey.

"Come," said John to everyone gathered around him, "come and repent for all the wrong things you have done!"

John was baptizing people in the River Jordan and telling them about Jesus.

"Someone very special is coming, and you need to repent," John told the crowd. "I am preparing the way for Jesus so that you will know Him when He comes. He is much greater than I am."

TALK TIME
The word "repent" means saying sorry, and doing wrong is called sinning. Have you ever said a prayer to Jesus saying sorry for anything that you have done wrong?

PRAYER TIME
Dear Jesus, today I want to come to you and say sorry for the things that I have done wrong. They are.................. Will you please forgive me? Amen.

BIBLE TIME
Matthew 3: verses 13-17

God's son

Jesus knew that John was baptizing people in the River Jordan and wanted to be baptized, too. By doing this, Jesus was giving His life to His Heavenly Father.

John the Baptist gently lowered Jesus into the water. As He came up, the Spirit of God came down from Heaven upon Him just like a dove and rested on Him.

God's voice could be heard from Heaven. He said, "This is my son whom I love. I am very pleased with Him."

Now Jesus was ready to do the work that His Heavenly Father wanted Him to do.

TALK TIME
Talk about how you see God as your Heavenly Father.

PRAYER TIME
Thank you, Jesus, that you obeyed your Father in Heaven and that He made you ready for all the things He wanted you to do. Thank you, too, that you're my Father in Heaven. Amen.

BIBLE TIME
Luke 5: verses 1-3

Teaching by the lake

Jesus lived and taught by the Sea of Galilee. One day he was teaching a big crowd of people about God's Kingdom.

Because everyone wanted to hear what Jesus was saying, they pushed forward to get closer to the front. There were SO many people.

Then Jesus had an idea. He saw two boats by the lake that had been left by the fishermen as they washed their nets.

"Can I get into one of your boats?" he asked them. They nodded. Jesus hopped into the boat and the fishermen pushed Him out onto the lake from the crowds.

Now Jesus could teach much better to the people. His voice could be heard by everyone.

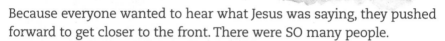

TALK TIME
Have you ever been among a big crowd of people? How did you feel?

PRAYER TIME
Dear Jesus, you always know the best way to talk to us so that we can hear you better. Thank you that you got into that boat so that you could speak to the crowds better. Amen.

BIBLE TIME
Luke 5: verses 4-6

Catching fish

When Jesus finished teaching He spoke to the fishermen.

"Go into deep water and put your net over the side to catch fish," He said to them.

One of them, a fisherman named Peter, smiled and said, "We've been fishing all night and haven't caught a thing! But I will do as you ask."

Peter threw the net over the side and waited... slowly, he began to pull the net up.

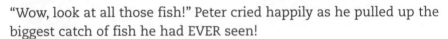

"Wow, look at all those fish!" Peter cried happily as he pulled up the biggest catch of fish he had EVER seen!

TALK TIME
Has Jesus ever given you a big surprise? Perhaps an answer to prayer? Talk about it.

PRAYER TIME
Dear Jesus, thank you for the wonderful surprise that you gave Peter. Thank you for the surprises you give me, too. Amen.

BIBLE TIME
Luke 5: verses 7-10

Just TOO many

Peter was astounded with all the fish in his net. He was struggling to collect them all. His net was breaking beneath the weight. So he called the other fishermen to help him.

They pulled and pulled the nets. Fish were jumping everywhere. It all began to get too heavy in the boat with so many fish, and it nearly sank.

Peter looked at Jesus and trembled, "Only God could have done all this," he said, before falling on his knees.

The other fishermen were also trembling. They knew it was God that had helped them catch so many fish.

TALK TIME
If you were on the boat, what would you have thought?

PRAYER TIME
Dear Jesus, help me to see when you do big things in my life. Amen.

BIBLE TIME
Luke 5: verses 10-11

Follow me

After the fishermen had caught so many fish, they pulled the boats up on the shore. Peter and all his fishermen friends were still amazed at what had happened with the big catch of fish.

"Don't be afraid," said Jesus. "I need friends like you. I need help in teaching people about the Kingdom of God. Come, follow me."

The fishermen looked at their boats and then looked at Jesus. It was an easy decision to make. They put their nets aside and pulled up their boat upon the shore.

They knew they wanted to follow Jesus and to become His disciples.

TALK TIME
"Disciple" means a follower of Jesus.
Explain how you would like to follow Jesus.

PRAYER TIME
Dear Jesus, please help me to follow you all of my life, just like your fishermen friends did. Amen.

BIBLE TIME
John 2: verses 1-2

A wedding

Jesus, His disciples, and
His mother were all
invited to a wedding.
The wedding was in a
town called Cana,
which wasn't too far
from the Sea of Galilee.

Everyone had been busy for
weeks preparing for the
wedding. There was food to
be made, dresses to be sewn,
drink to be delivered, flowers to
be arranged, and tables to be
decorated. All the guests were excited
about going to the wedding.
It was going to be a very wonderful celebration!

TALK TIME
*Have you been to a wedding? What do you think is important
about a wedding?*

PRAYER TIME
*Dear Jesus, thank you for all brides and grooms getting married
today. Please help them have a happy time on their wedding
day. Amen.*

BIBLE TIME
John 2: verses 3-5

No drinks

At last the day of the wedding arrived. Many guests arrived along with Jesus, His disciples, and His mother.

Everyone was having a good time talking and eating. The bride looked lovely in her beautiful wedding dress.

Suddenly Jesus' mother noticed that the wine had run out. Oh no... what a terrible thing to happen at a wedding!

She whispered to Jesus, "There is no more wine."

Some servants were standing nearby and she turned to them and said, "When Jesus asks you to do something, please do it."

TALK TIME
What can you think of that would be a disaster at a party?

PRAYER TIME
Dear Jesus, thank you that out of a disaster you can make everything all right. Amen.

BIBLE TIME
John 2, verses 6-8

Puzzled servants...

O no! All the drink had run out at the wedding! Jesus turned to the servants and instructed them, "You see those six huge water jars? Please fill them up with water."

The servants went backwards and forwards carrying large jugs of water and started to fill the water jars up. Finally, all of the jars were full to the brim.

"Now," said Jesus to a servant, "take a glass from one of the jars and give it to the master of the wedding." The servant was puzzled. Why take just water when it should be wine at a wedding?

TALK TIME
Have you ever been puzzled when someone has asked you to do something and you're not sure why? What did you say?

PRAYER TIME
Dear Jesus, thank you that you knew all along what you were doing at the wedding, and you wanted to show your power. Amen.

BIBLE TIME
John 2: verses 9-11

The best ever!

Jesus asked a servant to take a glass of water from one of the jars to the master of the wedding.

"Please could you taste this," said the servant, still a bit puzzled that it should be wine and not water.

The master of the wedding sipped from the glass. After tasting it, he exclaimed, "This is the best wine I have ever tasted! Wherever did it come from?" he asked.

The servants were even more puzzled. How had the water become wine? The disciples looked at Jesus and knew that Jesus had done a miracle!

Jesus had changed the water into wine!

TALK TIME
This was the first miracle of Jesus. What do you think the servants and the disciples thought?

PRAYER TIME
Dear Jesus, thank you for your first miracle! It must have been a very special day for the people at the wedding. Amen.

BIBLE TIME
Luke 8, verses 22-23

Calm waters...

Jesus had been busy teaching crowds and crowds of people and needed a rest. It was a perfect sunny day.

"Let's get in a boat," suggested Jesus, "and sail to the other side of the lake."

So His disciples and Jesus got into a boat and settled down. They put the sails up... it was a perfect day to go sailing. Jesus needed the calm water of the sea so He could rest for a while.

Jesus lay down in the back of the boat and closed His eyes, and the boat drifted across the lake quietly.

TALK TIME
Talk about ways you like to relax.

PRAYER TIME
Dear Lord Jesus, I was so glad to hear that you, too, got tired and needed a rest. I'm glad that you could close your eyes and rest for a while. Amen.

BIBLE TIME
Luke 8: verse 23

Bad weather

Because Jesus was so tired, He fell asleep on the boat... a much needed sleep. The disciples sailed the boat across the Sea of Galilee. The water was very calm.

But all of a sudden it wasn't quite so peaceful! A wind began to blow....dark clouds appeared over the hills by the lake. The water got choppy, and the small waves turned into big waves that started to rock the boat back and forth!

It began to get very, very stormy on the lake.

The disciples were frightened... but Jesus went on sleeping.

TALK TIME
Has there ever been a time you have been frightened when other people were not? When?

PRAYER TIME
Dear Lord Jesus, thank you that whenever I am in a storm you can give me your peace. Amen.

BIBLE TIME
Luke 8: verse 24

Frightened

"Jesus, Jesus!" the disciples cried in panic. "There is a terrible storm and we are all going to drown."

Jesus awoke, rubbed His eyes, and looked at His disciples. Slowly, He sat up and then stood up in the boat. Everyone else was falling. The storm was making the boat tip in all directions.

Suddenly, Jesus shouted, "You wind," He cried out, "STOP! You stormy waters... STOP."

And guess what?.. the wind stopped, the storm died down, and the water became calm again! The disciples looked in amazement, first at the calm waters... and then at Jesus.

TALK TIME
What do you like about stormy weather? What don't you like about it?

PRAYER TIME
Dear friend Jesus, it really is amazing how you speak and things happen! May I always be amazed when you speak to me. Amen.

BIBLE TIME
Luke 8: verse 25

Trust Jesus

The disciples were
surprised at what had happened.
Jesus calmed the storm before their very eyes.
Not only were they surprised, but they were frightened.

"Don't be frightened," Jesus said to them. "Just trust in me always.
See that the water is calm now. You don't ever have to worry... just
trust me."

The boat continued to sail across the lake just as it had before.
The disciples were in awe of Jesus. They saw even the weather
obeyed Him.

TALK TIME
Do you worry? What do you worry about?

PRAYER TIME
*Dear Lord Jesus, thank you that you are with me, and I can give
my worries to you. I always want to trust you, Jesus. Amen.*

BIBLE TIME
Luke 10: verses 38-40

Jesus visits

In a little village there lived two sisters, Martha and Mary. One day they heard that Jesus was coming to visit them.

"O my!" exclaimed Martha, "I must get some extra special food to make an extra special supper for Jesus. Then I must clean all of this house for Him."

There was a lot to be done before Jesus arrived.

She got out her broom and began to get very busy. Rush... rush... rush... sweep... sweep... cook... cook... cook.

Martha was very excited about her very special guest coming.

All day long she scrubbed, swept, and cooked.

TALK TIME
Do you like helping with the housework? What do you like doing best?

PRAYER TIME
Dear Jesus, help me not to rush about too much and make things more important than you. Amen.

MARTHA AND MARY   Day 231

BIBLE TIME
Luke 10: verse 39

Two sisters

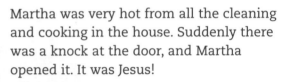

Martha was very hot from all the cleaning and cooking in the house. Suddenly there was a knock at the door, and Martha opened it. It was Jesus!

"Come in, dear Jesus," said Martha. "Please sit down, but excuse me a minute, I've just got to go and see to the meal." She hurried out to the kitchen.

Martha was getting even hotter from all the hard work that she had been doing. Martha was all hot and bothered!

Meanwhile, Mary just sat at the feet of Jesus and listened to Him talk.

TALK TIME
Talk about today's picture. What is happening to Martha and Mary?

PRAYER TIME
Dear Lord Jesus, thank you for your wonderful love whether we are too busy or not too busy. Amen.

BIBLE TIME
Luke 10: verse 40

Very annoyed

Martha rushed around trying to get the meal ready.

Mary sat at the feet of Jesus, listening to Him talk.

Martha glanced around the door and saw Mary and Jesus talking together. She became even hotter, not from working too hard now, but from annoyance.

"Jesus," she wailed, "can you tell my sister not to just sit there... tell her to come and help me NOW! I've got SO much to do in the kitchen!"

TALK TIME
Have you ever been annoyed when someone hasn't helped you? What happened?

PRAYER TIME
Dear Jesus, please help me not to get annoyed and angry. Please help me to have your peace. Amen.

BIBLE TIME
Luke 10: verse 40

Sit peacefully

"I'm doing all this work by myself," cried Martha, "and Mary just sits at your feet doing nothing!"

"Martha, Martha," said Jesus calmly. "Put down all your work. Come and sit here."

Jesus told Martha that He was very thankful for all the hard work that she had done preparing for His visit. All these things are important, He said. "But sometimes," Jesus continued, "it's better to come and sit at my feet just like Mary and talk and listen to me."

TALK TIME
Do you ever sit still and listen to or read about Jesus instead of being busy?

PRAYER TIME
Dear Jesus, teach me to listen to you sometimes when I am too busy doing things. Amen.

BIBLE TIME
Matthew 18: verse 1

Who is it?

All the disciples were together.
They had been talking about which
of them was the greatest in God's
Kingdom.

"Who could it be?" they asked.
"Who is the most well known and
greatest among us?" they
questioned. They went on discussing,
but they just ended up having an
argument between themselves.

"I know," said one disciple. "Let's
ask Jesus. He'll know who is the
best person among us."

They called Jesus over to their group.

"Which one of us do you think is the most
important?" they asked Him.

TALK TIME
Do you know people who think they are important?

PRAYER TIME
*Dear Jesus, help me not to think that I am too important.
Help me to keep my eyes on you. Thank you that I am special
to you. Amen.*

BIBLE TIME
Matthew 18: verses 2-5

A little child

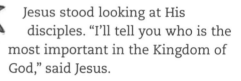

Jesus stood looking at His disciples. "I'll tell you who is the most important in the Kingdom of God," said Jesus.

He saw a little child and beckoned to him. "Come," He said to the child, "join us over here."

Jesus looked at His disciples again and then at the child.

"You will all need to change," He told them. "I love the simple faith and trust of little children. You will need to be like this child here... he is the greatest in the Kingdom of God."

The disciples stood still listening to Jesus. The child just looked up into the face of Jesus.

TALK TIME
Why do you think Jesus said this?

PRAYER TIME
Dear Lord Jesus, thank you that you love children everywhere. Thank you that you love me. Amen.

BIBLE TIME
Mark 10: verse 13

Children come to Jesus

Jesus had been preaching, teaching, and traveling from place to place. It had been a busy time for Him. Moms and dads would bring their children to Him so that He could bless them.

Jesus would gently place His hands on their heads and say a prayer of blessing.

The children loved Jesus. He was kind, thoughtful, and caring. He loved each one of them and said that no one should stop the children coming to Him.

TALK TIME
Can you think of a blessing that Jesus would have given to the children?

PRAYER TIME
Dear friend Jesus, thank you that you are such a blessing to children. I always want to come to you because you are gentle and loving. Amen.

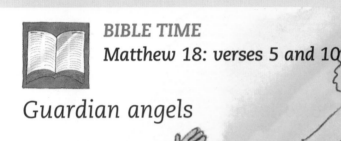

BIBLE TIME
Matthew 18: verses 5 and 10

Guardian angels

Jesus looked at the child that stood with Him and told the disciples, "You must welcome children, for they are very important and precious in my Kingdom."

Jesus wanted the disciples to know that if they welcomed children, they welcomed Him.

"Don't ever overlook or reject children," He continued, "for the angels in Heaven know each one of them by name and take care of them."

TALK TIME
How do you feel about an angel looking after you?

PRAYER TIME
Thank you, dear Jesus, that you give an angel to look after each one of us. Amen.

BIBLE TIME
Matthew 6: verse 9

Our Father in Heaven

All of the disciples were sitting with Jesus.
It was a prayer time, and Jesus was praying.
When He had finished, one of the disciples asked Him, "Jesus, can you teach us to pray, too?"

So Jesus began to teach them by saying, "Start off by saying 'Our Father in heaven...'"

Jesus wanted everyone to know that there is a Father in heaven who loves them on earth here and now and forever more.

TALK TIME
Don't you think it's great that we have a Heavenly Father who is always there for us and loves us! How does this make you feel?

PRAYER TIME
Dear Jesus, thank you that we can all talk to our Father in Heaven. I'm so glad that He is always there for me. Amen.

BIBLE TIME
Matthew 6: verse 11

Provides

Jesus went on to teach His disciples more about prayer.

He said that they were to ask for their daily needs. Their Father in heaven knew what they needed to get through each day. It was very important not to ask for tomorrow... but only for today. It could be food, clothing, friendship, or even somewhere to live... but ask only what is needed for one day at a time.

TALK TIME
What are the needs of your family?

PRAYER TIME
Dear Heavenly Father, thank you for providing for all my needs. Thank you for giving us what we need just for today. Amen.

BIBLE TIME
Matthew 6: verse 12

Forgive us and others

Jesus wanted to teach more on prayer. The disciples were listening to Jesus very carefully as He explained how to pray.

"It is very important," He said, "to know that when you do something wrong each day you need to ask your Father in heaven for forgiveness. None of you is perfect, and each day you may hurt someone or say something hurtful."

He told them that they should say sorry to God if they have hurt someone.

Jesus also said, "You also need to be able to forgive someone who has hurt you. Maybe someone has done or said something wrong to you."

TALK TIME
Can you read or have someone read to you the scripture verses for today? Has someone hurt you recently? Talk about it.

PRAYER TIME
Dear Jesus, please help me when I get hurt. Please also help me to forgive the person who hurt me. Amen.

BIBLE TIME
Matthew 22: verse 35

Best law ever?

A group of people who were experts on the laws in Israel asked Jesus a question.

"What is the most important thing in life?" they asked.

"Love the Lord with all of your heart, soul, and mind," Jesus replied.

They were amazed at Jesus' teaching.

Then Jesus said that there was also another law and told the group, "You must love other people more than yourself."

TALK TIME
Do you let Jesus know how much you love him? How?

PRAYER TIME
Dear Jesus, I love you so very much. Thank you for your teaching. Help me to love other people more than myself. Amen.

BIBLE TIME
Luke 12: verses 22-24

Do not worry

All the disciples were gathered around Jesus. They loved to hear Him teach.

Jesus looked at them and said, "Don't worry about your life. Don't worry about what you are going to eat or wear, because," said Jesus, "life is much more important than worrying. Look at the birds in the air," he told them, "they don't have stores of food or houses... yet look how their Heavenly Father looks after them."

TALK TIME
What are some of the things that you need today?

PRAYER TIME
Dear Jesus, I'm so happy that you know what I need from day to day. Thank you for looking after me. Amen.

BIBLE TIME
Luke 12: verses 27-28

Have faith

Jesus went on teaching His disciples.

He pointed to some beautiful flowers in a field and said, "Look how those lilies grow. Aren't they beautiful?" The disciples looked at them. Then Jesus continued, "The lilies don't have to work hard to look beautiful. God gave them beauty when they grow in the fields."

Jesus then said that if God did this for a lily in the field... how much more would God provide for His people.

He looked at His disciples. "You must seek God first," he told them, "and then God will take care of you."

TALK TIME
Talk about ways that you learn about Jesus during the day.

PRAYER TIME
Dear Jesus, I want to be able to seek you in all ways so that my faith will grow. Please will you help me to do this? Thank you for your for what you provide. Amen.

BIBLE TIME
Luke 12: verses 32-34

Treasure in Heaven

Again Jesus looked at His disciples.

"Don't ever be afraid," he said gently, "for what you seek from your Heavenly Father, He will give to you."

"But," Jesus went on to teach them, "don't seek treasures of the world. Give to the poor. Have a 'heavenly purse' so that you will give to others and not keep things for yourself."

"Keep on having faith in God," Jesus said. "For He knows your needs, and He will want you to store up treasure in heaven by giving to others."

TALK TIME

"Treasures in heaven" are things you do for God and other people. Talk about what you do regarding treasures in heaven.

PRAYER TIME

Dear Lord Jesus, thank you that you see the ways I give and sometimes what I don't give! Thank you that you see and know everything. Help me to store up heavenly treasures. Amen.

BIBLE TIME
Mark 5: verses 21-23

Jairus' daughter

A huge crowd had gathered around Jesus. He had already done so many miracles that everyone wanted to see Him heal more people.

Suddenly, out of the crowd came a man pushing his way toward Jesus.

The man's name was Jairus, and he was the head of the local synagogue, which is like a church.

Jairus fell down at Jesus' feet.

"Please come to my house," he cried. "My daughter is very ill and might die. She is only twelve years old. I know you can make her better."

TALK TIME
Do you know of anyone who is ill? Have you ever been very sick? Did someone pray for you?

PRAYER TIME
Dear Jesus, Please make............... feel better. Thank you, Jesus, that we can ask you to make them feel better. Amen.

BIBLE TIME
Mark 5: verses 24-32

Jesus follows Jairus...

"Of course I will come to your home and see your daughter!"
He said. "Show me the way to your house!" and started making his
way through the crowds. Suddenly He stood still.

"Someone touched me," He said.

"Someone very ill touched me and has been healed.
Someone touched me because I felt the power rush out from me."
The disciples were amazed at Jesus.

TALK TIME
Talk about how Jesus is never too busy for people.

PRAYER TIME
*Dear Jesus, thank you that you always have time for each
one of us. Amen.*

BIBLE TIME
Mark 5: verses 33-34

It's me

Someone had touched the hem of Jesus' robe.

Jesus looked around the crowds to see who had touched Him.

He knew that whoever it was had been healed.

"It's me," said a woman timidly as she pushed her way forward. She fell at Jesus' feet and said, "I have been ill for such a long time, and I knew that if I could touch even the hem of your robe, I would be healed."

Jesus lovingly looked at the woman.

"You trusted me to heal you. Now go in peace. You are completely better."

The woman smiled a huge smile at Jesus! She was happy that Jesus had healed her.

TALK TIME
What a miracle! Do you know of someone in your church who has been healed?

PRAYER TIME
Dear Jesus, thank you that the woman was so happy when you healed her. Amen.

BIBLE TIME
Mark 5: verses 35-36

Have faith

Jesus was on his way to Jairus' house to heal his daughter. All of a sudden some men pushed through the crowd to Jesus. They had run all the way from Jairus' house.

"Don't bother to go to the house now," they panted. "Jairus' daughter is dead."

The crowd hushed and grew silent... all eyes were on Jesus.

Poor Jairus! Jesus looked at him and gently said, "It'll be all right... just trust and have faith in me."

TALK TIME
Why would Jairus have faith in Jesus?

PRAYER TIME
Dear Jesus, help me to trust and have faith in you just like the woman who touched your robe and like Jairus who asked for his daughter to be healed. Amen.

BIBLE TIME
Mark 5: verses 37-39

Unbelief

Jesus set off toward Jairus' house with three of His disciples, Peter, James, and John. When they arrived at the house, there was another crowd. All of them were wailing and weeping very loudly. The sad news of the death of Jairus' daughter had spread very quickly. All of the crowd were upset.

"Why are you all crying?" asked Jesus. "There's no need to be upset. The girl is not dead... she's only sleeping!"

The crowd laughed, "But we've seen her... and she's most certainly dead!"

TALK TIME
If you had been there, what would you have said to Jesus?

PRAYER TIME
Dear Lord Jesus, I am so glad that you are always in control of everything and know exactly what is happening. Amen.

BIBLE TIME
Mark 5: verses 40-41

Jesus speaks

Jesus told everyone to move out of the way because He wanted to go into Jairus' house. The crowd still believed that the little girl was dead.

"We know she has died," the crowd shouted and continued to cry.

Jesus entered the house with the father and mother and the three disciples. Together they went to the room where the girl was lying. She certainly looked dead. She wasn't moving at all.

But Jesus knew that He could perform a miracle.

He knelt down where she was lying and looked very tenderly at the little girl. He took hold of her hand and said, "Little girl, get up!"

TALK TIME
What do you think the mother and father thought when Jesus said this to the little girl?

PRAYER TIME
Dear Jesus, I love to read about how you perform miracles and how you heal people. Amen.

BIBLE TIME
Mark 5: verses 42-43

Healed and eating!

As soon as Jesus spoke to the little girl, she opened her eyes. She had come back to life!

Immediately, she threw back her bed covering and stood up. Her parents were amazed and gasped. They ran toward their daughter and hugged her. What a miracle! Their little girl had been healed.

The little girl looked at her parents and said to them, "I'm hungry."

So Jesus said, "Go and get a meal for your daughter."

They immediately prepared the finest food for their daughter. The mother and father were full of joy and praised Jesus for healing their precious daughter.

TALK TIME
Can you think of ways to praise Jesus?

PRAYER TIME
Thank you, Jesus, that you gave so much joy to this family because you healed the little girl. Amen.

BIBLE TIME
Luke 5: verses 12-13

Please heal me

Jesus was walking through a town when a man came up to Him.

He had sores all over his body. The man was very ill with a disease called leprosy.

He fell down in front of Jesus and begged Him, "Jesus, if you are willing, please heal me."

Jesus looked at the man with love. He reached out His hand to the man and said, "I am willing to heal you. Be healed now."

Immediately all the sores left the man's body, his skin became clear, and the leprosy disappeared! The man was overjoyed that he had been healed and praised Jesus.

TALK TIME
When Jesus heals people, what do they immediately want to do?

PRAYER TIME
Dear Lord Jesus, I want to praise you for all the ways that you make people feel better, and how you heal them. Amen.

BIBLE TIME
Luke 17: verses 11-13

Ten of them

Jesus was walking towards Jerusalem. As He approached the city, He saw ten men. They were all ill because they had leprosy. Their bodies were covered with sores. They were left alone because people thought that if they came near, they would get leprosy, too. The lepers stood at a distance from Jesus and called out to Him.

"Jesus," they said, "have pity on us." Jesus went over to them.

"Go and show yourselves to the priests." That's all He said to them!

As the lepers made their way to the priests, they were healed!

TALK TIME
Another miracle! Why do you think the ten men were healed?

PRAYER TIME
Jesus, thank you that you healed so long ago and you also heal today. I want to praise you. Amen.

BIBLE TIME
Luke 17: verses 15-19

Saying "thank you"

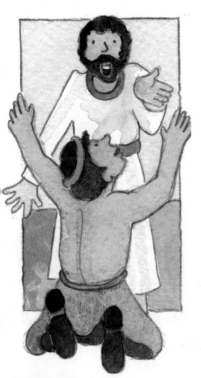

One of the ten healed lepers was so grateful to Jesus that he decided to return and thank Him.

He walked back singing and praising. He saw Jesus and fell at His feet.

"Thank you, Jesus, for healing me. I'm so grateful to you."

"That's good that you returned to thank me. Where are the other nine men I healed?" asked Jesus.

They were nowhere to be seen.

It was so sad that only one of the lepers returned to thank Jesus.

TALK TIME
When Jesus has answered your prayers, do you thank Him? What has He done for you recently?

PRAYER TIME
Dear Jesus, thank you that you have answered my prayers. Please forgive me if I haven't returned to say thank you. Amen.

BIBLE TIME
Luke 5: verses 17-18

Such excitement

One day Jesus was teaching in a house. People had gathered from many villages around to hear Him. Even some great teachers of the law had come to hear Him.

Everyone tried to squeeze into the house. They were excited to hear Jesus teach.

Outside the house there was a man who desperately wanted to be healed. He couldn't walk at all and was lying on a stretcher.

"Please," he begged to some friends, "take me to see Jesus."

TALK TIME
Do you get excited when Jesus teaches you something? What would you have felt if you were in the crowd?

PRAYER TIME
Dear Jesus, I want to be excited when I see you move among people, teaching and healing them. Amen.

Through the roof

The lame man's friends picked up the man on the stretcher.

They tried to get to the door, but there were so many people they couldn't even reach the door – let alone get inside the house!

"I know," said a quick-thinking friend, "let's go on top of the roof and see if we can get to Jesus that way."

So they climbed up to the roof with their friend on the stretcher.

TALK TIME
What do you like about this story?

PRAYER TIME
Dear Lord Jesus, I am so excited to be able to see you every day. Help me find ways to do this. Amen.

BIBLE TIME
Luke 5: verses 18-19

Letting him down

The men scrambled onto the roof carrying their lame friend on the stretcher. Now, all they had to do was somehow lower him into the house so that Jesus could heal him.

They decided to make a hole in the roof, so they began removing the tiles. Dust fell on the heads of the people below. Everyone was amazed. It seemed like the roof was falling in on them!

When the hole was big enough, the men gently lowered their friend on the stretcher down among the crowd.

Jesus just stood there looking. Whatever was going to happen next?

TALK TIME
Have you ever had an adventure with someone?

PRAYER TIME
Thank you Jesus. It is always an adventure when I walk with you day by day. Amen.

Jesus heals

Suddenly with a "BUMP" the lame man landed right near to where Jesus was standing in the crowd. Jesus didn't seem surprised at all. He just laid His hand on the lame man's head.

"I have seen your trust in me," He said to the poor lame man. "Now all the wrong things you have done have been forgiven."

"Wait a minute!" yelled one of the teachers of the law angrily, "you can't say that. Only God can forgive!" The teachers of the law began to get angry with Jesus. "Who does He think He is?" they muttered.

TALK TIME
Do you know of anyone who doesn't believe in what Jesus can do? What would you like to say to them?

PRAYER TIME
Dear Jesus, I am so glad that I believe in all that you do. Please help me to tell other people all about you. Amen.

BIBLE TIME
Luke 5: verses 23-26

Get up and walk

Jesus saw that the men of the law did not like Him doing miracles. He had just healed a lame man, and they were very angry.

Jesus looked at them and calmly said, "I want to show you men of the law that God has given me power not only to forgive but also to heal." He then turned to the lame man on the stretcher and said, "Get up and walk!"

Immediately, the man stood up in front of the crowds, rolled up his stretcher, and walked from the house, praising God.

Everyone in the house was amazed at Jesus.

TALK TIME
Say something that has amazed you about Jesus.

PRAYER TIME
I'm so glad that you still amaze me today, Jesus, with your wonderful miracles. Amen.

BIBLE TIME
John 9: verses 1-3

Born blind

One day as Jesus and His disciples walked along a road, they came across a blind man begging.

The beggar had been born blind.

"Jesus," the disciples asked, "this man who was born blind, did it happen because his parents had done wrong?"

"No," replied Jesus, "God doesn't punish people by making their children blind. But God uses the blindness to show how powerful He is."

TALK TIME
Can you guess what happens next?

PRAYER TIME
Dear Jesus, you love people so much that you always want to touch them in a special and powerful way. Amen.

BIBLE TIME
John 9: verse 6

Mud!

Then Jesus walked over to the blind man.

The disciples looked on, watching.

Jesus knelt down and spat on the ground. He then mixed together a bit of the dry mud and His spit. The disciples looked on with amazement at what Jesus was doing.

Then He rubbed the little bit of wet mud onto the blind man's eyes. The disciples looked on with even more amazement!

"Go now," said Jesus to the blind man, "and wash your face in the Pool of Siloam."

TALK TIME
What would you have thought if you were there with the disciples?

PRAYER TIME
Dear Jesus, sometimes even when I don't understand why you do things... I want to trust you. Amen.

BIBLE TIME
John 9: verses 7-9

I can see!

So the blind man hurried off to the Pool of Siloam, still with the mud on his eyes.

He came to the pool, and he bent down to wash his eyes just as Jesus had asked him to do.

SPLASH! SPLASH! SPLASH! He felt his face becoming clean as he wiped the mud off. He then shook the water from his face and opened his eyes... WOW... he could see!

His neighbors were even more surprised.

"Isn't that the blind man who used to beg?" they asked. "No, no," others said, "it only looks like him."

"It is me!" said the healed man. "I met a man named Jesus, and He has given me back my sight. Isn't it wonderful!"

TALK TIME
What do you like about this story?

PRAYER TIME
Dear Jesus, thank you that you made this blind man see so that others would know your power of healing. Amen.

BIBLE TIME
John 4: verses 45-47

A royal officer

Jesus was visiting Galilee. All the people there welcomed Him. They had heard about the great miracles He had done. The good news about Jesus spread fast!

Not far away, there lived a royal officer whose son was very ill. When the royal officer heard that Jesus was in town, he went to find Him.

On seeing Jesus he begged, "Please come and heal my son. He is very close to death. I want him to be well again."

TALK TIME
How do you think the royal officer felt when he found Jesus?

PRAYER TIME
Dear Jesus, I love the way people gather around you and expect BIG things to happen. Amen.

BIBLE TIME
John 4: verses 48-50

Seeing miracles

Jesus looked at the royal officer and began to speak. He wanted the crowd to hear Him too, "I know you all want to see wonders and miracles... and that is right... but I also know if you see wonders and miracles, you will believe in God."

The royal officer again pleaded with Jesus. "Please sir, please come quickly, my child is dying."

Then Jesus replied, "You may go, for your son will live. He is healed." The royal officer hesitated for a moment and then went on his way back home.

TALK TIME
*Jesus wanted the royal officer to have faith in Him.
Talk about your faith in Jesus.*

PRAYER TIME
*Dear Jesus, please teach me to have more faith in you every day.
Amen.*

BIBLE TIME
John 4: verses 51-53

They believed

On his way back home the royal officer's servants came running down the road to greet him.

"It's all right," they yelled. "Your son is alive. He has recovered!"

The royal officer asked them, "What time was he healed?"

The servants told him the exact time. The royal officer knew it was the exact same time that Jesus had said to him and to the crowd that his son would recover!

Then everyone rejoiced at what had happened... they knew that Jesus had healed the boy. Because of this the whole household believed in Jesus.

TALK TIME
Why do you think Jesus does miracles?

PRAYER TIME
Dear Jesus, thank you for your miracles. Thank you that everyone believed when they knew it was you who performed the miracles. Amen.

BIBLE TIME
John 11: verses 1-2

Brother of Mary and Martha

In a little village named Bethany lived Mary and Martha and their brother Lazarus. One day Lazarus became very, very ill.

Mary and Martha didn't think that their brother would live very long. They knew that Jesus loved Lazarus and that Jesus would be able to make him better.

So they sent a message to Jesus.

"Please come quickly and help Lazarus. He is very ill."

When Jesus heard the message He said, "Don't worry, Lazarus won't die. Something will happen next that will make people want to praise God the Father and His son."

TALK TIME
Why do you think Jesus wanted His name and His Father God's name to be praised?

PRAYER TIME
Dear Lord Jesus, when I see you moving in people's lives, it makes me want to praise your name. Amen.

BIBLE TIME
John 11: verse 5

Jesus stays away

Mary and Martha waited and waited for Jesus to arrive. They wanted him to be with their ill brother Lazarus. For two whole days they waited. During this time Lazarus became more and more ill.

Mary and Martha couldn't understand why Jesus hadn't come immediately.

Back in Jerusalem Jesus told His disciples that Lazarus was going to die, but something special would happen so that they would believe in His power.

"It is important that I am not with Lazarus at the moment," He explained to them.

TALK TIME
What would you have thought if you were with Martha and Mary?

PRAYER TIME
Dear Jesus, help me to understand that you always have perfect timing when you want to do something special. Amen.

BIBLE TIME
John 11: verses 17-21

Comfort from neighbors

Lazarus became even more ill and then died.

Poor Mary and Martha felt so sad. Many of their neighbors came to their home to comfort them. They cried and cried, for they had lost a very dear brother.

It was the custom in those days to put the body immediately into a grave. So they wrapped Lazarus' body up in strips of linen and placed him in a tomb.

A few days later Jesus arrived at Mary and Martha's house.

Martha ran to meet him. Although she was pleased to see him, she cried, "My brother is dead. Why didn't you come sooner?"

TALK TIME

Jesus always has perfect timing. Have you ever been late for something? Did you get told off?

PRAYER TIME

Dear Lord Jesus, teach me always to know your perfect timing. Amen.

BIBLE TIME
John 11: *verses 21-27*

Lazarus is dead

"Jesus," cried Martha, "where have you been? We sent a message to you for you to come immediately. If you had come earlier Lazarus wouldn't have died."

Martha was very upset that Jesus had arrived too late. Jesus had compassion for Martha and simply told her, "Your brother will come alive again, Martha."

"Oh, I know he will be alive in heaven," she replied.

"Anyone who believes in me will always live," Jesus said. "Do you believe this, Martha?"

"Yes," said Martha, "I do believe in all that you say, for you are the son of God."

TALK TIME

Can you look up the word "compassion" in a dictionary? What does it mean?

PRAYER TIME

Dear Jesus, thank you that you came into the world to do wonderful things and show us that you are the Son of God. Amen.

BIBLE TIME
John 11: verses 28-32

Jesus cries

When Martha had spoken to Jesus about Lazarus, she went back to their home to call her sister, Mary.

"Jesus is here," she said, "and He's asking for you."

Mary got up quickly and ran to meet Him. The neighbors who had been comforting Martha followed behind her.

When Mary saw Jesus, she fell down at His feet weeping and crying.

All of the neighbors began to cry. Their loving brother and friend, Lazarus, had gone, and they missed him so much.

Jesus was moved by their sorrow and sadness, and He cried, too.

TALK TIME
Had you ever thought about Jesus crying because He was sad? What do you think about this?

PRAYER TIME
Dear Jesus, knowing that you cry too helps me to understand how you feel. Amen.

BIBLE TIME
John 11: verses 36-38

See how He loves

Lazarus was dead, and Mary and Martha were crying. The neighbors stood around and spoke among themselves.

"See how much Jesus loves Martha and Mary and how He misses His friend Lazarus, too," they said.

"But," said others, "if He's healed blind men, why did He let Lazarus die?" They just couldn't understand what was going on.

Jesus was deeply moved by the people and their sadness. He went toward the tomb where Lazarus lay dead.

"Take away the stone," He yelled.

Everyone gasped... what on earth was He doing!

TALK TIME
When you feel sad or upset, who do you like to comfort you?

PRAYER TIME
Dear Jesus, thank you that you cried with Martha and Mary and felt their sadness. Thank you that sometimes when I'm sad, you comfort me. Amen.

BIBLE TIME
John 11: verses 39-40

Roll the stone away

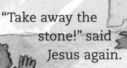

"Take away the stone!" said Jesus again.

"Oh, no," wept Martha, "you can't take away the stone now, Jesus. Lazarus has been dead for four days. His body will be smelly." All the neighbors watched. They remained still and silent and just looked at Jesus and Martha.

"Did I not tell you, Martha," Jesus said to her, "if you believe... Lazarus will come alive again?" Martha nodded.

"I want you to see the glory of God working," Jesus said.

The neighbors rolled the stone away. They were wondering what Jesus was going to do next.

TALK TIME
If you had been there, would you have believed that Jesus could make Lazarus come alive again? Why?

PRAYER TIME
Dear Lord Jesus, I praise you for what you were about to do with Lazarus. I praise you that Mary and Martha and all the neighbors waited expectantly to see your power. Amen.

BIBLE TIME
John 11: verses 41-44

Lazarus comes alive!

"Father in heaven," Jesus said, "I want everyone here to believe in you."

Then Jesus looked at the tomb and said, "Come out, Lazarus!"

Slowly the dead man rose and came out of the tomb still wrapped in the strips of linen.

The crowd gasped...

"Lazarus is alive!" They looked in amazement.

Jesus said very quietly to them, "Take off the strips of linen and let Lazarus walk."

They did as He asked.

Everyone there who saw Lazarus dead and then come to life believed in Jesus.

TALK TIME
What do you like best when you hear about Jesus healing people?

PRAYER TIME
Dear Lord Jesus, I am really amazed at all of the healings that you do and all the people you have helped. Thank you for healing them. Amen.

BIBLE TIME
Mark 6: verses 30-32

Peace and quiet

Many people were following Jesus, because they had heard about His teaching and how He healed many people.

Jesus and the disciples had been so busy with the crowds that they hadn't found time to even eat. They were getting very hungry!

"Come," said Jesus. "Let's go and find a place were we can find some rest."

So Jesus and His disciples found a boat, and they all clambered on board. They rowed to the other side of the Lake of Galilee where they hoped they would find some peace and quiet.

TALK TIME
If you want peace and quiet, where do you go and why?

PRAYER TIME
Dear Jesus, it's good to know that you wanted peace. Help me to find peace and be with you. Amen.

BIBLE TIME
Mark 6: verses 33-34

Racing to find Him

The crowds saw Jesus and His disciples row away in the boat. They wanted to be with Jesus and hear all that He taught. They also wanted to see more healings. So the crowd left the town and ran around the edge of the lake to the other side. They arrived just before Jesus and His disciples got there in the boat.

The crowd was excited that they had just managed to catch up with Him... now surely He would teach them again and heal some more people!

Jesus got out of the boat and looked at the crowd. Even though He was very tired, He loved each one of them. He didn't want to turn any of them away.

TALK TIME
What do you like about Jesus?

PRAYER TIME
Dear Jesus, you wanted some peace and quiet, but you still had time for all the people. I want to thank you for wanting to be with me, too. Amen.

BIBLE TIME
Mark 6: verse 34

Jesus teaches

A very large crowd had gathered around Him at the water's edge. They pushed and jostled to be near Him.

"I hope He is going to teach us today," said one of the onlookers.

"I wonder what He will teach us?" said another.

"Do you think He will heal somebody today?" asked someone.

"What wise words do you think He will tell us?" said someone else.

And so Jesus began to teach them more. The crowd loved to listen to Him.

That day He taught them many things. By the time Jesus had finished teaching, it was very late in the day.

TALK TIME
Which stories do you like to hear about Jesus?

PRAYER TIME
Dear Jesus, thank you for teaching us. I love to listen to you always. Amen.

BIBLE TIME
John 6: verses 5-9

Feeding time

All day the crowd had been listening to Jesus teach, and now the evening had come.

"Everyone is hungry!" said Jesus. "Where shall we go and buy some food for everyone to eat?" Jesus asked His disciples.

"WHAT!" exclaimed one disciple. "It would take more than eight months' wages to feed this crowd today. There are thousands of people here!"

"Wait a minute," said another disciple. "There is a young boy here, and he has some food... five small loaves and two small fish. But I don't think that will feed many people!"

TALK TIME
What do you like to take with you when you go on a picnic?

PRAYER TIME
Dear Jesus, thank you that you already knew how you were going to feed all of the people. Thank you for your miracles. Amen.

BIBLE TIME
John 6: verses 9-11

Saying grace

The young boy stood in front of Jesus holding the small basket with five loaves and two fish in it. He was willing to give his small portion of food to Jesus to be shared among the crowd.

Jesus then said to His disciples, "Tell the people to sit down on the grass."

So the disciples turned to the crowd and motioned with their hands for everyone to sit down.

What was Jesus going to do next, they wondered?

Jesus took the basket from the small boy. He held it up and said "thank you" to His Heavenly Father for the five small loaves and two fish.

TALK TIME
Saying a prayer before a meal is "a grace". What grace do you like saying before you eat?

PRAYER TIME
Dear heavenly Father, thank you for this boy giving Jesus his only food. Thank you for all the food you provide for us day by day. Amen.

BIBLE TIME
John 6: verses 11-13

Full up!

Everyone was then handed some fish and bread... more than five thousand people had something to eat that day. What a big crowd!

They ate, they chatted, and they all enjoyed the food. What a lovely day it had been.

When they were all full, Jesus instructed His disciples, "Now I want you to go and gather all that has been left over. Pick it all up. I don't want you to waste anything."

So the disciples did as Jesus asked. They went among the people and picked up the leftovers and filled twelve baskets full!

Everyone knew that Jesus had given them a miracle that day.

TALK TIME
If you had been there, what would you have enjoyed?

PRAYER TIME
Dear Jesus, thank you for the picnic miracle. Thank you that people love to see you perform miracles. Amen.

BIBLE TIME

Luke 19: verses 1-2

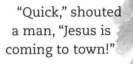

Jesus is coming...!

"Quick," shouted a man, "Jesus is coming to town!"

Jesus was on His way to Jericho, and the word had got around very quickly that He was coming. People began to hurriedly gather in the center of town to catch a glimpse of Him.

"There He is!" yelled another. "He's arrived."

The people's excitement rose. The people of Jericho had high hopes of having Jesus in their town. They had heard about His teaching and miracles.

"Hurry," said someone else, "we don't want to miss Him!"

TALK TIME

If you were in Jericho, how would you have felt when you heard that Jesus was coming?

PRAYER TIME

I always want to be excited about you, Jesus. May others around me see this and want to know all about you. Amen.

BIBLE TIME
Luke 19: verse 2

Money, money, money

Everyone was running to meet Jesus... everyone except one man. He was a little man. No one in the town liked him. His name was Zacchaeus, and he was the town's tax collector.

He collected money from people, but he always collected too much from them. Zacchaeus was a very rich man on their money. They all hated him because he was a cheat!

There were lines of people along the road to see Jesus, and Zacchaeus wanted to see Him, too.

TALK TIME
Have you ever wished that you were either taller or smaller?

PRAYER TIME
Dear Lord Jesus, let me be happy with how you made me because you love me as I am. Amen.

BIBLE TIME
Luke 19: verse 4

Zacchaeus finds a way

Zacchaeus tried to see over people's heads, but he was too short. Suddenly, Zacchaeus had an idea. He saw a very large tree. It was a tall sycamore tree which had big branches. He ran over to it and started to climb. Up and up he climbed. It was a good spot to see Jesus from and, what's more, he couldn't be seen by the people who didn't like him!

He settled down on one of the wide branches and drew back some of the leaves so he was able to peer down.

At last he could see Jesus coming... Zacchaeus was so excited!

TALK TIME
Do you have any good ideas? What are they?

PRAYER TIME
Dear Jesus, thank you that Zacchaeus found a way to see you, for it was very important that you wanted to meet with him that day. Amen.

BIBLE TIME
Luke 19: verse 5

Come for dinner

As Jesus walked through the crowds, people cheered and clapped Him.

They thought it was very special to see Jesus; they'd heard all about the miracles He had done.

"Welcome to Jericho!" they shouted.

Jesus saw Zacchaeus in the tree and said, "Come down! I want to eat at your house tonight."

TALK TIME
How do you think Zacchaeus felt, getting an invitation from Jesus?

PRAYER TIME
Dear Lord Jesus, Thank you that you love each one of us... even Zacchaeus. Amen.

BIBLE TIME
Luke 19: verses 5-6

He fell with a shock

Zacchaeus couldn't believe it... an invitation to eat with Jesus! Him... Zacchaeus! Why, he wasn't good enough to be in Jesus' company let alone eat with Him!

Nor could all the people near the tree believe it.

"Zacchaeus," somebody exclaimed, "eat with Jesus? Surely not!"

"Jesus wants to eat with the cheat," shouted another. "There must be some mistake."

Zacchaeus was as shocked as the rest of the crowd... why would Jesus want to eat with someone as bad as he?

He fell out of the tree with surprise and landed at Jesus' feet.

TALK TIME
Why did you think Jesus invited Zacchaeus to eat with Him?

PRAYER TIME
Dear Jesus, it was wonderful to hear that you wanted to eat with Zacchaeus, even though others didn't like him. Thank you that you invited him. Amen.

BIBLE TIME
Luke 19: verses 6-7

Moan... moan... moan

Jesus looked at Zacchaeus on the ground. He quickly jumped up, and Jesus stepped toward him joyfully.

"Now look," cried one of the onlookers, "Jesus is even talking to the cheat."

"Jesus is going to a sinner's house," moaned another. "Why didn't He ask one of us instead?"

"Zacchaeus has taken all of our money, and now he gets the best invitation from Jesus," complained someone else in the crowd. "It's not fair!"

The crowd went on moaning and moaning about all that they had seen with Jesus and Zacchaeus.

TALK TIME
Have you ever moaned or said, "It's not fair" about anything? What was it? How did it work out?

PRAYER TIME
Dear Jesus, help me never to be selfish and moan about things. Help me to see what you are doing instead. Amen.

BIBLE TIME
Luke 19: verse 8

I'm changing!

Zacchaeus was happy to be in the company of Jesus. Why... he felt so proud to be walking with Him! But being with Jesus made Zacchaeus realize that he had done so much wrong in his life. He had cheated all the people in Jericho out of their money... and suddenly he felt very guilty.

"Jesus," he said, looking at Him, "I have been so bad, and I want to change things! I'm so sorry that I have cheated people, and I want to pay them back four times the amount I have taken from them. What's more, I want to give half of my belongings to the poor."

The crowd around couldn't believe what Zacchaeus had just said!

TALK TIME
What do you think about Zacchaeus saying this?

PRAYER TIME
Dear Jesus, I'm so happy that you changed Zacchaeus. Thank you that you can change each one of us with your love. Amen.

Everyone is happy

The crowds were shocked... was Zacchaeus really offering to give money back to them?...unbelieveable!

Never in their whole lives had they seen anyone like Zacchaeus change so much. They stood with their mouths wide open.

Zacchaeus stood and looked at Jesus... his new friend. There was silence, and then Jesus spoke.

"Don't you see what has happened?" he said to the crowd. "My Heavenly Father has sent me to the world to share His love, even to those who have done bad things. Today Zacchaeus found that love."

TALK TIME
Has Jesus' love touched your life? How?

PRAYER TIME
Jesus, you knew all along that Zacchaeus' life would be changed. Thank you for touching my life with your love. Amen.

BIBLE TIME
Luke 15: verses 1-2

Lost sheep

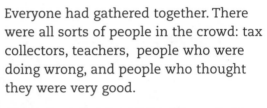

Everyone had gathered together. There were all sorts of people in the crowd: tax collectors, teachers, people who were doing wrong, and people who thought they were very good.

"I don't understand it!' said one. "This man Jesus eats with bad people."

"Also," said one of the bad ones, "He welcomes them with open arms and talks to them!"

Jesus just sat there listening.

He then turned to the crowd and started to teach them a parable, which is a story giving a lesson.

"Just suppose," he began, "you were a shepherd looking after a hundred sheep..."

TALK TIME
Do you know why Jesus sat with people who did wrong?

PRAYER TIME
Dear Jesus, I am so glad you gather together all sorts of people because you love them. Amen.

BIBLE TIME
Luke 15: verse 4

Counting sheep

"This shepherd," continued Jesus with the parable, "knew every one of his hundred sheep well. He knew what they all looked like, their color, and even the way they walked! Every night he would call out to them and gather them up. He would then guide them toward the pen where they would be safe in the dark from prowling animals. Every night he would count them as they entered the pen. But one night there was a problem. The shepherd stood counting each sheep as they passed him... he got up to ninety-nine and looked around for the last sheep, but it was nowhere to be seen! Now the first thing a shepherd feels when he knows there is a sheep missing is sadness. And this shepherd was sad."

TALK TIME
What are things that make Jesus sad?

PRAYER TIME
Dear Jesus, I am like one of your sheep, and you are my shepherd. Thank you that you gather me up and keep me safe. Amen.

BIBLE TIME
Luke 15: verse 4

Looking for the lost

"This shepherd," said Jesus, "cared so much for that one lost sheep. He quickly locked the door to the pen to keep all the others sheep safe for the night. He then picked up his stick and went to look for that one lost sheep. He hunted and hunted, he looked and he looked, he crossed fields and hills and searched and searched. He shouted and shouted, he looked behind rocks, and he looked behind bushes.

He looked everywhere for that one lost sheep."

TALK TIME
Do you think Jesus is like this shepherd when He looks for us?

PRAYER TIME
Dear Jesus, I am so glad that you are like this shepherd who searched and searched for me. Amen.

BIBLE TIME
Luke 15: verses 5-6

Found at last!

Jesus continued the story.

"Finally, after searching and searching, the shepherd found the lost sheep. The shepherd was overjoyed and happy, and the sheep was, too. He was so glad to see his shepherd coming toward him; he'd felt so lonely and lost without him. The shepherd put the sheep on his shoulders and started to walk back to the pen. They both arrived back, and the shepherd put the sheep among the others... he was safe at last! Now this sheep could sleep peacefully all night... he had been lost, but his shepherd had found him."

TALK TIME
What do you like about this parable?

PRAYER TIME
Dear Jesus, thank you that you found me and put me into your family. Amen.

God searches

After telling the crowd the parable about the sheep, Jesus turned to the crowds and said to them, "I mix and talk with people who are not good because God is like that shepherd. Many people have gone missing, and God cares so much about them that He will go searching for them everywhere until He finds them."

Jesus continued, "When one person, who hasn't been very good, is found by God and says that they are sorry for the bad things they have done, I tell you the whole of heaven has a party because that one missing person has been found!"

TALK TIME
Re-read the story of the sheep on Day 291 and imagine you are the lost sheep.

PRAYER TIME
Dear Shepherd Jesus, I'm so glad that you found me, and now I am safe with you. Thank you that you are my shepherd. Amen.

BIBLE TIME
Luke 14: verses 16-17

A big party

Jesus wanted to tell the crowd another parable. So he told them about a very rich man who wanted to give a big party.

"There was a man," said Jesus, "who ordered all of his servants to do all the organizing of the party. So they swept the floor and polished and dusted everything. The servants prepared and cooked the very best of foods. It all smelled and looked wonderful. They laid the tables with very expensive plates and drinking glasses. There were colorful flowers put around the room. Everything was ready for the party. The rich man was pleased with everything that had been done."

TALK TIME
What do you do when you get ready to go a party or give a party?

PRAYER TIME
Dear Lord Jesus, thank you so much for all the excitement I feel when going to a party or when I give a party. Amen.

BIBLE TIME
Luke 14: verse 17

Invitation sent out...

Jesus continued with the story...

"The rich man looked around the room where his party was to

be held. The servants had worked so well and everything looked welcoming. 'Well now,' said the rich man, 'everything is ready to start the party.'

So he asked one of servants to go out to the village and invite people to his very grand party. So off went the servant. He knocked at the first door. 'Come,' said the servant, 'my master is having a great party, and you are invited.'"

TALK TIME
What's the best party you have ever been to?

PRAYER TIME
Dear Lord, thank you for all the wonderful parties everywhere and that you love us to have fun. Amen.

BIBLE TIME
Luke 14: verses 18-19

Excuses, excuses

"'Can you come to the party?' asked the servant. The first guest came to the door. He had a worried look on his face. 'I would love to come to the party but I am SO sorry! I have just bought a piece of land, and I must go and see that it's all right.' The servant turned away disappointed. He went on to the next house and knocked on the door. 'Come,' he said, 'my master is having a party, and you are invited.' But this man was like the first guest who was invited. 'I'm SO sorry,' he said. 'I have just bought some cows, and I must go and see that they're all right.' The servant turned away extremely disappointed."

TALK TIME
Do you know anyone who has made excuses for something? What did they say?

PRAYER TIME
Dear Jesus, I'm so sorry you feel disappointed when someone makes an excuse not to follow you. Amen.

BIBLE TIME
Luke 15: verses 20-21

More excuses

"The servant continued to ask other people to come to the party. 'Please come,' he begged a guest. 'My master is having a party, and you are invited.' The next guest looked at the servant and said, 'SO sorry, I can't come. I've just been married and I'm far too busy.' The servant was very disappointed. He had asked several people, and they had all made excuses. He walked back home. He found his master and reported what had happened. 'I have knocked on doors and invited so many people to the party, but each one of them has said they couldn't come.' The master became very angry because the guests had turned down his invitation."

TALK TIME
Have you ever made an excuse? What was it for?

PRAYER TIME
Dear Jesus, help me always to be kind to friends and family and not make them sad or disappointed when I can't do what they ask. Amen.

BIBLE TIME
Luke 14: verse 21

Invite others...

"'Look at all the lovely things we have made ready for a wonderful party, and no one has bothered to come,' said the rich man angrily. 'We'll have to invite other people.' He then had a brilliant idea. He called his servant again and said, 'Go quickly into the streets and alleys of the town and invite the poor, the crippled, the sick, and the blind people.' So off went the servant to invite everyone he could find.

When all these people received the invitation to the party... they were happy to accept. They came in crowds to the rich man's house. They sat at the tables eating, drinking, chatting, and laughing. They were pleased to be joining in all the fun!"

TALK TIME
What do you like about today's reading?

PRAYER TIME
Dear Jesus, thank you that you look out for people who don't ever get invitations... but you invite them to be with you. Amen.

BIBLE TIME
Luke 14: verses 23-24

More at the party...

"'Sir,' said the servant, 'I have invited all those you wanted to be at your party, but there's still loads more food and more room at the tables.' 'Well, then,' said the master, 'go and invite people who would love to come to my party. Go into the countryside and ask others. I want my house to be full of people who would just love to be here at my party.' And so the servant went out again to invite more to the party, and loads more people came back with him to join in the fun of the party!"

TALK TIME
Talk about the difference in the first guests who turned down the invitation and the second guests who accepted the invitation.

PRAYER TIME
Dear Lord Jesus, thank you that you love to teach with parables. Thank you for this one about a party and for those who wanted to come. Amen.

BIBLE TIME
Luke 14: verse 24

Jesus' party

"The party was the best one that the guests had ever been to. They talked and laughed and ate as much of the delicious food as they could eat! The rich man was pleased that these people had accepted his invitation."

Jesus then said to the crowd who had been listening to his parable, "This is what it is like when God invites people to be with Him. He loves us all... the rich and the poor, the sick and the crippled, the well and the not so well. He wants to invite us all to His party, but we need to accept His invitation to be with Him.

TALK TIME
Jesus has invited you to be with Him each day. Will you go?

PRAYER TIME
Dear Jesus, thank you that when you invite us to be with you, we, too, can have such joy. I will go with you today. Amen.

BIBLE TIME
Luke 18: verse 9

Too good

Jesus wanted the crowds to know about people who think they are better than others. So He told another parable...

"There were two men praying at the temple. One of them thought that he was praying to God the right way. He was so sure that in the eyes of God he was very good. He prayed about himself, 'I'm so glad that I am not like other men. I am good. I'm so glad that I am not like men who do wrong things. I'm so good. I'm even glad that I am not like that tax collector over there!' And the man continued praying. 'God, I even fast for you and give some of my money over to you. I'm so good. Amen.'"

TALK TIME
What do you think about the way that this man prayed?

PRAYER TIME
Dear Lord, please help me not to think I'm too good at times. Amen.

BIBLE TIME
Luke 18: verse 13

Not so good!

"Not far away, also praying, was another man – the tax collector. He knew that he wasn't so good.

He couldn't even look up to heaven as he didn't think himself worthy but kept his head bowed. 'O Lord, have pity on me,' he prayed. 'I have been bad. Please have pity on me. In your eyes I have not obeyed you and have turned my back on you. Please have mercy on me.' This man beat his fists on his chest in sorrow because he thought he had made God sad. 'Please God, forgive me, have pity on me.'"

TALK TIME
What do you think about the way that this man prayed?

PRAYER TIME
Dear Lord, thank you for this man who prayed to you. How much you must love him for his honesty. Amen.

BIBLE TIME
Luke 18: verse 14

Humble

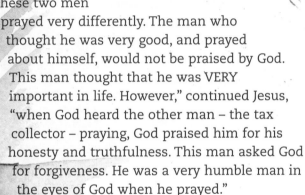

Jesus looked at the crowd and said to them, "I tell you the truth, these two men prayed very differently. The man who thought he was very good, and prayed about himself, would not be praised by God. This man thought that he was VERY important in life. However," continued Jesus, "when God heard the other man – the tax collector – praying, God praised him for his honesty and truthfulness. This man asked God for forgiveness. He was a very humble man in the eyes of God when he prayed."

TALK TIME
'Humble" means not making yourself important to God or people. Do you know any people like this?

PRAYER TIME
Dear Lord Jesus, teach me not to make myself important in front of you and other people. Amen.

BIBLE TIME
Matthew 13: verses 31-32

It is so BIG

Jesus wanted to
teach the crowd
what Heaven was like.
So he said to the people,
"Heaven is like a mustard seed!"
And he continued,
"A man took this tiny, tiny seed
and planted it in his field. He
watered it, and it began to
grow. From the tiniest of
seeds a huge big tree grew.
It was so HUGE that even
the birds could come and
perch on the branches and
have protection in this tree.
And that is what heaven is like!"

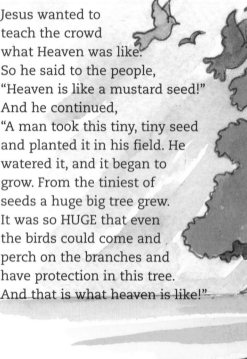

TALK TIME
What else do you think heaven will be like?

PRAYER TIME
*Dear Jesus, thank you for heaven and for showing me how big
and safe it is... just like that HUGE tree. Amen.*

BIBLE TIME
Luke 15: verses 11-12

A sad suggestion

Jesus had been teaching the crowds again. He wanted to tell them a very special story about a son who went against his own father. Only later on the son became very sorry for what he had done.

"There was a father," started Jesus, "who had two sons. He loved them both very much. But one day, the younger son came to his father with a suggestion that made him very sad. 'Father,' he said, 'one day when you die, I will have half of your money... but the thing is, I want it now to enjoy my life while I'm young. Can I have the money now?'"

TALK TIME
Can you talk about how you have to wait for something?
Do you get impatient?

PRAYER TIME
Dear Jesus, please let me think before I ask for something. Sometimes the things I ask for are things that are not important. Please forgive me. Amen.

BIBLE TIME
Luke 15: verses 12-14

Gimme, gimme

"So the father sadly gave his youngest son all that belonged to him. The young man tied up the money in bags and put them around his waist. He was so excited to be off on his travels! He wanted to find out about the world and what was happening in far distant places. He couldn't wait to leave his parents and his older brother who looked after the boring farmland. He had a big, excited smile on his face. He was looking forward to meeting new and interesting people. As the young man left his family home, his father became even more sad. He wasn't even sure that he would ever see his young son again..."

TALK TIME
What do you think about this young man leaving home? Should he have done it? Why?

PRAYER TIME
Dear Jesus, please help me not to ask for the wrong things. Amen.

BIBLE TIME
Luke 15: verses 13-14

The wrong kind of excitement

"So the young son left his home, and off he went to discover new places. He found groups of people who loved him... but only for his money! He drank with them, he danced with them, he bought fine gifts for them. He even gambled his money. What fun he was having! He spent his money as fast as he could, and he wasn't very wise about how he spent it. But all of a sudden the money ran out... he had spent the entire amount! Slowly his friends left him, and he was all alone in the world."

TALK TIME

Why did these friends leave him? Were they good friends to have?

PRAYER TIME

Dear Jesus, help me to be very wise with my money and not be like this young man. Thank you for my friends. Help me to be a good friend to them. Amen.

BIBLE TIME
Luke 15: verses 14-17

A job?

"The young man didn't have a penny left in his pockets, and he began to panic! He was a long way from home, and now all of his friends had left him penniless. He was in a very poor state. 'I know,' he said. 'I'll go and get a job.' He went to look for one. Eventually, he got a job looking after pigs, feeding them and taking care of them. One day he was SO, so hungry that he even wanted to eat the food that he was giving to the pigs! But he wasn't just hungry, he was lonely, too. 'If only I hadn't left home,' he wailed."

TALK TIME
When this young man first left home, he was excited. Talk about how he felt when he first left home and how it turned out for him.

PRAYER TIME
Dear Lord Jesus, sometimes I do things when I shouldn't, and I get into a mess. Help me to be wise always. Amen.

BIBLE TIME
Luke 15: verses 17-19

So sorry

"'It's not fair,' cried the young man. 'I'm here starving to death all alone... and at home they're all having the best of everything... even my father's servants.' He shoved some food at the pigs to eat and felt very sorry for himself. Then he had a bright idea. 'I know,' he said to himself. 'I'll return home. I'll tell my father that I'm sorry for what I have done. I'll also tell him that it wasn't right to ask him for all that money. I'll go and say sorry to him and that I made a big mistake leaving home.' Once he'd made up his mind, the young man left his place of work and began to travel back home."

TALK TIME
Have you ever had to say sorry to someone? What happened?

PRAYER TIME
Dear Lord Jesus, I'm so sorry for all the wrong things I have done... even today. Please forgive me. Amen.

BIBLE TIME
Luke 15: verses 20-21

Welcome home

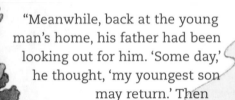

"Meanwhile, back at the young man's home, his father had been looking out for him. 'Some day,' he thought, 'my youngest son may return.' Then one day as he glanced down the road from his home, he saw a figure in the distance. Could it be...? Is it..? It may be...? Yes, it was... his long lost son! The father ran as fast as he could toward him... his son stood still as his father came closer. 'MY SON,' cried his father. 'You've come home!' He threw his arms around his young son and kissed him. 'Father,' the son said, 'I'm so sorry I have wasted your money. I have done so many things wrong, and I have lost all the money you gave me.'"

TALK TIME
What a loving father! Can you talk about the opposite way the father could have reacted?

PRAYER TIME
Dear heavenly Father, you long for us to come to you so that you can give us love as a Father. Thank you that you are always there waiting for us with your arms open wide to hug us. Amen.

BIBLE TIME
Luke 15: verses 22-24

Party time!

"The father was SO happy that his long lost son had returned and the son, too, was happy to be home. His father's welcome was so warm and loving despite his being very grubby and dirty. 'Quick!' said the father to the servants, 'bring the best clothes you can find. Put a ring on my son's finger and new sandals on his feet.' They did this at once, and the son looked smart once more. 'Let's have a party to celebrate,' said the father. 'My son who I thought was lost has been found again!' And that's what happened... everyone joined in the party and had fun."

TALK TIME
What do you like about this story?

PRAYER TIME
Dear Jesus, thank you for this son who returned home, and thank you for the father's welcome. Amen.

BIBLE TIME
Luke 15: verses 25-30

The other son

"Everyone was dancing and singing and welcoming the long lost son back home. People were eating the most wonderful food and drink... that is... nearly everyone. The older son didn't feel like celebrating. He was very angry. 'What's happening?' he asked. 'I have been here all the time, caring for the farm, looking after the animals, and working hard, and yet when my brother returns home after wasting my father's money and leading a very bad life... here you all are giving him a great welcome home with a party. What about me?'"

TALK TIME

When you have seen another person get something special, have you ever said, "But what about me?"?

PRAYER TIME

Dear Jesus, please help me to think of other people and not be selfish, thinking about my needs and wants. Amen.

BIBLE TIME
Luke 15: verses 31-32

The same love

"'My son, my son,' said the father putting his arm around the older son, 'I love you dearly. I have enjoyed and appreciated all the good things that you have done for me on the farm. You have worked very hard.' He then looked tenderly at his older son and explained. 'The reason why we are celebrating now is that I thought I would never see your brother again. But today we are all back together again as a family, and I am so grateful he has returned!'"

TALK TIME
Talk about times when you felt like the older brother – angry and left out. Can you go to your parents or caregiver and talk about it?

PRAYER TIME
Dear Lord Jesus, thank you for parents and caregivers all over the world. Thank you for the care they give. Amen.

BIBLE TIME
Luke 10: verses 25-30

Love your neighbor

Jesus was teaching again when a man among the crowds asked Him a question. "Can you tell me," he said, "what I must do to live forever?" Jesus looked at him and replied, "Love God with all of your heart, and love your neighbor as you love yourself."

"But who is my neighbor?" asked the man.

"Well," replied Jesus, "listen to this story and I will tell you."

Jesus started to tell another parable.

"There was a man who was traveling from Jerusalem to Jericho..."

TALK TIME
Do you love the Lord with all of your heart?

PRAYER TIME
Dear Jesus, thank you for all the beautiful and wonderful ways in which you give to me. I love you. Amen.

BIBLE TIME
Luke 10: verse 30

Robbers

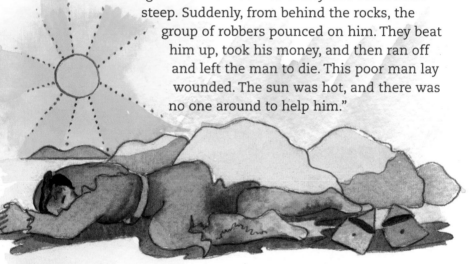

"Along the road from Jerusalem to Jericho," said Jesus, "a group of robbers lay waiting. They were very sly, nasty, and cruel. They hid behind a very large rock waiting to rob any travelers who passed by. One day, along this road came a man who was walking alone. The road was twisty and sometimes steep. Suddenly, from behind the rocks, the group of robbers pounced on him. They beat him up, took his money, and then ran off and left the man to die. This poor man lay wounded. The sun was hot, and there was no one around to help him."

TALK TIME
What do you think about these robbers?

PRAYER TIME
Dear Lord Jesus, please will you show robbers how much pain and hurt they leave behind them. Amen.

BIBLE TIME
Luke 10: verses 31-32

Pass on by

"A while later," continued Jesus,
"a priest, who worked in the temple,
was traveling down this same road. He came
around the bend of the road and saw the wounded
man. He didn't stop but just walked to the other
side of the road and continued walking. A little
later on, another man came by. He also served God in
the temple. Now, what do you think he did? Well, he,
too, just like the priest, walked on by and didn't stop
to help the poor wounded man."

TALK TIME
Can you think of someone who would like your help today?

PRAYER TIME
*Dear Jesus, please show me how to help people today who
need help. Amen.*

A KIND MAN

BIBLE TIME
Luke 10: verses 33-34

With love

"And so this poor injured man just lay there," continued Jesus. "No one helped him. Not long after these two men had passed him, a third man walked along the road. He was a Samaritan."

"A Samaritan!" shouted the crowd. "We hate the Samaritans!"

"Yes, I know," answered Jesus, "but this Samaritan was different than you think. He stopped when he saw the wounded man on the ground. He took pity on him and didn't pass him by like the other two. Instead, he knelt down by the side of the injured man, cleaned his wounds with a cloth, and put bandages on him."

TALK TIME
The Samaritans were from another part of the country. Jesus was teaching them to love one another. Talk about times when you felt Jesus was teaching you to love someone.

PRAYER TIME
Dear Lord Jesus, I want to learn to love my neighbors, friends, and other people as you love them. Please help me. Amen.

BIBLE TIME
Luke 10: verses 34-35

Such care

"Then," continued Jesus, "after bandaging the wounded man and giving him a drink, he brought his own donkey, put the injured man on its back, and led him along the road. With the man safe and comfortable on his donkey, they walked some distance. Further along the road the Samaritan found a hotel. He stopped and carried the wounded man inside and laid him down. 'Please take care of this man,' said the Samaritan to the hotel keeper. He also paid the hotel keeper some money so that the injured man could stay at the hotel."

TALK TIME
What do you like about this story so far?

PRAYER TIME
Dear Jesus, thank you for this kind Samaritan who took care of the injured man. Thank you that you also take care of us very gently and tenderly. Amen.

BIBLE TIME
Luke 10: verses 36-37

Who is the best neighbor?

Jesus was teaching about the Samaritan and the wounded man because He wanted people to know who their neighbors are and to love them.

Jesus then looked at the man who had asked Him a question in the beginning, and asked "So, who do you think is the best neighbor... the two that walked past the injured man or the third man who stopped and helped him?"

"The third one," said the man. This was the Samaritan who had helped the wounded man.

"That's right," answered Jesus. "A neighbor is anyone who needs your help. Now go and help someone today."

TALK TIME
Is there a neighbor of yours in need today? What can you do for your neighbor?

PRAYER TIME
Dear Lord Jesus, thank you for your stories that teach us how to behave and love one another. Amen.

BIBLE TIME
Matthew 13: verses 1-3

Sowing seeds

Jesus was sitting beside the sea, and a huge crowd had gathered to hear Him teach. Jesus wanted to teach them a story about believing in Him and His Heavenly Father. So He started to tell them,

"One day a farmer went to sow some seeds. He scattered some seeds from his bag, and they fell onto the pathway. Some birds came flying down and ate the seeds all up. The sower threw out some more seeds and these fell on rocky ground. There wasn't much soil there for the seeds to grow. Because they couldn't put their roots down deep enough, the seeds sprang up and soon died because there wasn't enough soil for them to grow."

TALK TIME

Have you ever planted seeds? What did you plant? Did you look after them so they could grow?

PRAYER TIME

Dear Lord Jesus, thank you that you gave us fields and gardens to grow things in. Amen.

BIBLE TIME
Matthew 13: verses 7-8

Sowing

Jesus continued to teach.

"The sower threw more seeds on the ground, but these fell among many thorns. The seeds started to grow, but they were choked by the thorns around them. They soon withered and died. However, some of the seeds that the sower planted fell onto some very good soil. Gradually these seeds grew and grew and grew and became very healthy plants."

TALK TIME
Have you ever seen a field full of corn or wheat?
What did you like about it?

PRAYER TIME
Dear Jesus, please let the words from your Bible grow in my heart so I will be healthy in you. Amen.

BIBLE TIME
Matthew 13: verses 10 and 18-21

The meaning of the seeds

The disciples asked Jesus what His story of sowing seeds meant.

"Well," answered Jesus, "this story means that many people will hear the truth of me and of my Heavenly Father, but each person will receive it differently. The seed sown along the pathway that is eaten by the birds is like the person who hears the good news of me and my Father... but the enemy of God, that is Satan, will come and snatch it away. The seed grown on rocky ground is like the person who receives the good news of me and my Father but it only lasts for a short time, because it didn't go deep into their hearts."

TALK TIME
Talk about the good news of Jesus. Do you ever talk to your friends about Jesus?

PRAYER TIME
Dear Lord Jesus, please help me to tell your good news and all that you have done. Amen.

BIBLE TIME
Matthew 13: verse 22

A worrier

"Now," said Jesus, "the seed that was planted in among all the thorn bushes tried to grow. It tried to grow among the thorns... but it failed. This," continued Jesus, "is like a person who hears the good news of me, then gets weighed down and choked with all the worries of the world. This person becomes too worried to bother with the good news that I am giving and is caught up in everyday worries that will stop him seeing me."

TALK TIME
Do you worry? What do you worry about? Talk about it.

PRAYER TIME
Dear Jesus, I'll try not to worry. Please forgive me when I do. Help me to give my worries over to you. Amen.

BIBLE TIME
Matthew 13: verse 23

Good soil

"But," said Jesus, "the seed that fell on the good earth is like a person who hears the good news of me and my Father and understands it! He will then go out and tell more people about us and make a wonderful harvest of people who will believe in me. This person will grow in the light and truth of all that I have taught them and will tell many, many other people about me and they will also come to believe in me and my Father."

TALK TIME
Talk with Jesus about the kind of person you would like to be and why.

PRAYER TIME
Dear Lord Jesus, help me to know you in a much deeper way... just like the seed that fell on the good soil. Amen.

BIBLE TIME
Matthew 14: verses 22-24

Being alone

Jesus had been teaching the crowds. It had been another busy day for Him and His disciples.

"Let's go over to the other side of the lake," said Jesus to His disciples, "but you go ahead of me in a boat because I want to be by myself... I want to pray."

So the disciples got into a boat and pushed it out onto the water. Jesus wanted to be alone with His Heavenly Father to talk to Him and be with Him.

So He made His way up one of the hills that surrounded the lake, to pray.

TALK TIME
Is there is a special place where you like to be alone so that you can talk to Jesus? Where is it?

PRAYER TIME
Dear Lord Jesus, help me have time to talk to you away from my busy daily life and be alone with you. Amen.

BIBLE TIME
Matthew 14: verses 24-26

A storm

On the mountainside Jesus began talking to His Heavenly Father.

Meanwhile, the disciples were sailing across the lake. They were far off from the land, and it was beginning to get dark.

A wind started to blow. It blew stronger and stronger, rocking the boat. A storm was brewing, and the disciples were beginning to get very frightened. The sea was now very rough.

Suddenly, out of the evening light, they saw a figure walking on the water... they became even more frightened!

TALK TIME
Have you ever been frightened? What happened? Who comforted you?

PRAYER TIME
Dear Lord Jesus, I know I don't need to be frightened because you are always with me. Help me to understand that. Amen.

BIBLE TIME
Matthew 14: verses 26-29

It's Jesus!

The disciples peered through
the stormy weather from their
boat. They were being rocked from
side to side with the huge waves.

But wait a minute... were they seeing
things?.. was that really a figure they
could see walking on the water? They panicked and
were filled with fear! Then a voice called to them,

"Don't be frightened; don't be afraid."

Peter, one of the disciples, recognized the voice
immediately.

"JESUS!" he shouted, "is that really you?
If you tell me to walk on the water I will
come and greet you."

"Come," Jesus replied to Peter.

TALK TIME
*Has there ever been a time when you have been frightened,
but you knew that Jesus was asking you to be with Him?*

PRAYER TIME
*Dear Jesus, when I am frightened, just like Peter, may I hear
your quiet, gentle voice saying, "Come to me." Amen.*

BIBLE TIME
Matthew 14: verses 29-30

Sinking!

Peter was so glad to hear the gentle voice of Jesus through the stormy, rough weather. All he wanted was to be safe with Jesus.

So without thinking he quickly jumped out of the boat and began walking on the water toward Jesus, who was waiting for him with open arms.

But then Peter became aware of the storm around him with the wind blowing, the stormy sea, and the waves that were SO big. It all was too much for him... and he began to sink.

He shouted out, "Save me, Jesus, save me!"

TALK TIME
Why do you think Peter was able to walk on the water?

PRAYER TIME
Dear Lord Jesus, I'm so glad that you are always there with your arms wide open when we are frightened. Amen.

BIBLE TIME
Matthew 14: verse 31

His arms

Poor Peter, he was frightened that he might drown in the water. He wanted to be with Jesus and walk to Him through the storm. But now he felt he was going to drown. Suddenly, a hand caught hold of his... it was strong. The hand began to slowly pull him up out of the stormy water... it was Jesus! Peter was so happy!

Jesus said to him, "When you started to walk on the water and got frightened, why didn't you believe that I would save you from the storm? Don't ever doubt that I can save you when things aren't going well for you."

TALK TIME
Do you believe that Jesus will always come to your rescue?

PRAYER TIME
Dear Jesus, thank you that you will always rescue me when things get tough. Amen.

BIBLE TIME
Matthew 14: verses 32-33

The Son of God

Jesus held Peter in His arms... the wind was still blowing and the water was still very rough.

They gradually got back into the boat with Jesus carrying Peter.

The disciples had been watching... and they were amazed at what they had just seen.

As Jesus and Peter climbed back into the boat, the wind slowly died down, and the water became calm.

The disciples looked at Jesus with such wonder and amazement that they started worshipping him saying, "Jesus, surely you are the Son of God!"

TALK TIME
When you worship Jesus, what do you say?

PRAYER TIME
Dear Jesus, I worship you in wonder, dear Jesus, at all the wonderful things you do... but most of all for saving me. Amen.

BIBLE TIME
Matthew 14: verse 34

They know Jesus

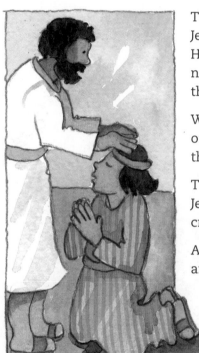

The disciples were so glad that Jesus was with them in the boat. How peaceful it was on the water now. The storm had died down, and they gently sailed on the lake.

When they reached the other side of the lake, they all climbed out of the boat.

The word quickly got around that Jesus had arrived on the shore. Soon crowds gathered to be with Him.

Among the crowds were sick people and disabled people, some with many illnesses. They all came wanting to be made better.

Jesus prayed with them, and they were all healed.

TALK TIME
What do you think about Jesus healing so many people?

PRAYER TIME
Dear Lord Jesus, I love to hear how you heal so many people. Thank you for touching all the sick, disabled, and ill people. Amen.

BIBLE TIME
Luke 18: verses 31-34

Don't understand

As Jesus sat with all of His friends He began to speak to them. "Very soon," He said, "we will be going to Jerusalem."

All the disciples listened to Him carefully. "And in Jerusalem," continued Jesus "some people who hate me will come for me. They won't be very nice to me and will do horrible things. I will die, but," said Jesus, "on the third day I will come alive again."

The disciples didn't understand what Jesus was talking about at all.

TALK TIME
Has there ever been a time when you haven't understood something? Did you ask a parent or friend to explain?

PRAYER TIME
Dear Lord Jesus, thank you for giving me parents, friends, and other people I can talk to when I have a problem. Amen.

BIBLE TIME
Matthew 21: verses 1-16

A Big Parade

Jesus said to His friends, "Let's go to Jerusalem now because soon something very important is going to happen!" So the twelve friends gathered up their belongings and walked with Jesus. On the way Jesus turned to two of His friends and asked them to go on ahead and borrow a donkey. They were to bring it back to where they would all be waiting.

Some time later, the two friends arrived back, and a cloak was put on the donkey's back. Jesus then got on the donkey and rode on the pathway toward the city of Jerusalem. His friends followed, wondering what was going to happen.

"Very soon," said Jesus, "there is going to be a big parade and celebration. Just stay with me."

TALK TIME
Do you ever wonder about things? What?

PRAYER TIME
Dear Jesus, you knew what was going to happen to you all along. I think it would have been so exciting to be with you on that parade. Amen.

BIBLE TIME
Mark 11: verse 9

Hooray for Jesus

As Jesus and His friends approached Jerusalem, people started to follow them. They were shouting with joy, "Hooray, here comes the King," and "Welcome Jesus," and "Blessed are you, Jesus, who comes in the name of the Lord!"

All the people marched alongside Him waving palm branches and laying them on the ground in front of the donkey. And soon a very large crowd had gathered and followed Jesus. They clapped, they cheered, and they sang. The crowd was so pleased to see Jesus coming into the city of Jerusalem.

TALK TIME
Today, this parade is called Palm Sunday. Could you draw a picture of how you would like to celebrate this day?

PRAYER TIME
Dear Jesus, Hooray! What a great procession into Jerusalem for you, Jesus! It's because you are our King and Lord. Amen.

BIBLE TIME

**John 12: verse 37
and verses 43-46**

Hating Jesus

Now in Jerusalem there were some men who didn't like Jesus. They disliked His teaching to the people, the miracles that had happened, and all the healings He had done.

They also hated how the crowds followed Him, cheering. They were very jealous and didn't believe in anything Jesus did.

They talked and discussed among themselves how they could get rid of Him.

These men liked only to get praises from people rather than God. But Jesus could see into their hearts and knew this.

So He said to them, "I have come into the world as a light so that people would believe in me and my Father in Heaven who has sent me. So let the crowds celebrate me coming into Jerusalem."

TALK TIME

Do you know anyone who doesn't know Jesus? What would you like to say to them?

PRAYER TIME

Dear Jesus, I am so thankful that I am learning about you day by day and that you are in my heart. Thank you that the crowd in Jerusalem loved you like I love you. Amen.

BIBLE TIME
Luke 22: verse 1-6

Not a friend

A very special day was coming: it was a festival called the Passover. Now there were men who hated Jesus, and they were looking for ways to get rid of Him. But because they were very important men, they couldn't do it themselves.

Judas, one of Jesus' friends, heard that a group was plotting against Jesus and so he went to meet the group and said to them, "What will you give me for helping to get rid of Jesus?" The men in Jerusalem were delighted that they had found someone to help them. They agreed to give Judas some money for helping them.

TALK TIME
Judas was going to betray Jesus. Look up the word "betrayed" and see the meaning of it.

PRAYER TIME
Dear Jesus, help me to be always a good friend and not disappoint my friends. Please teach me how to help them always. Amen.

BIBLE TIME

Matthew 26: verses 20-25;
John 13

Very sad

It was the Passover. Jesus was having a meal
with His disciples, and He spoke to them
again. "I'm going away tomorrow," he said. "I will
be sad to leave you, but I am going to be with
my Father in Heaven."

The disciples didn't understand what He
meant, but Jesus continued, "There is a
group of men in Jerusalem who want to
get rid of me." Jesus paused... "and one
of my friends here will betray me."
There was a gasp from his friends.
They couldn't believe anyone
would do such a thing to Jesus.
Then one of them, Judas, said,
"Surely not I, Jesus?"

And Jesus replied to him, "Yes,
it is you." Judas left the room immediately.

TALK TIME

Judas had let Jesus down. Has there ever been a friend who let
you down or disappointed you? What happened?

PRAYER TIME

Dear Jesus, thank you Jesus that even though Judas turned
against you, you still loved him as one of your friends. Amen

BIBLE TIME
Mark 14: verses 22-26

Bread and wine

During the Passover meal Jesus wanted to say more to His disciples.

"I want to share something with you," He said. Then He broke off a piece of bread and said thank you for all the food. Then He passed some of the bread to His disciples saying, "When you eat this bread, it is my body. Please, when you eat it... remember me." Jesus then said thank you for the wine and passed that to His disciples saying, "When you drink this wine it is my blood... remember me."

TALK TIME
Have you ever seen people at church take the bread and the wine? Can you say what happens?

PRAYER TIME
Dear Jesus, thank you for giving this very special time of taking the bread and wine with you. We remember you especially at this time, and what you have done for us. Amen.

BIBLE TIME
Mark 14: verses 27-31

Never!

Jesus looked at His friends and said, "Before the morning, you, my friends, will also turn against me."

"Oh, never!" cried Peter. "I would never do that. I will go anywhere with you, Jesus. I will always follow you wherever you go."

Jesus turned to Peter and said, "Tomorrow, very early in the morning, you will say you don't know me three times, and immediately afterwards you will hear a rooster crow."

But Peter was sure he would never, never let Jesus down.

TALK TIME

What do you think about Peter promising Jesus that he would never let Him down? Have you ever made a promise to someone and then found you couldn't keep it?

PRAYER TIME

Dear Lord Jesus, please always help me to keep the promises I make to my friends. Amen.

BIBLE TIME
Matthew 26: verses 36-45

Jesus prays

After the Passover meal, Jesus and some of His friends found a quiet place. It was called Gethsemane.

"Sit here and pray," Jesus told them. "I am going over there by myself to pray to my Heavenly Father."

And so Jesus went a little way away from them to be alone and pray. Jesus knew what was going to happen to Him in the next few days, and He was fearful.

After a while Jesus returned to His friends and found them sleeping! Jesus said to them, "Please pray. The friend who has turned against me is about to come, and I must do what my heavenly Father has told me."

Still His disciples didn't understand what Jesus was saying.

TALK TIME
When you pray, do you have a favorite prayer?

PRAYER TIME
Dear Jesus, help me never to give up talking to you. Today I pray for.......................... Amen.

BIBLE TIME
Matthew 26: verses 47-53

Danger for Jesus

Jesus was standing and talking to His disciples when suddenly
Judas, the friend who turned against Jesus, arrived. He had with him
some soldiers and a group of leaders from Jerusalem.

Judas said to the soldier quietly, "The man I give a greeting kiss to
is the man you arrest."

As Judas went toward Jesus, the soldiers also came forward and
grabbed hold of him. Jesus' friends looked on with horror. They were
frightened and ran away.

TALK TIME
*Look at Day 338 to see what Jesus said to His disciples. How do
you think Jesus felt at this time? Has a friend ever run away
from you?*

PRAYER TIME
*Dear Jesus, I feel very sad that your friends ran away from you.
Help me never to run away from you. Amen.*

BIBLE TIME
Mark 14: verses 53-65

Jesus is laughed at

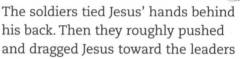

The soldiers tied Jesus' hands behind his back. Then they roughly pushed and dragged Jesus toward the leaders in Jerusalem. These men were very jealous of Jesus.

Jesus stood before the leaders.

"Ha, Ha!" one of them said. "He says He is a king of our people!"

They pointed their fingers at Him and laughed.

"And another thing," one of them shouted, "He says He will destroy our temple!"

They pointed their fingers at Him and laughed. "He says He is the Son of God."

They mocked and judged Jesus. Jesus stood silently in front of them. He knew all the things they were saying were true, but these leaders didn't believe them.

TALK TIME
It's not very nice to be laughed at. Has anyone laughed at you? How did you feel?

PRAYER TIME
Dear King Jesus, I am so hurt that these men did this to you. Help me never to point a finger at anyone or laugh at them. Amen.

BIBLE TIME
Mark 15: verses 66-72

A rooster crows!

After Jesus was arrested, Peter, the disciple, was warming himself by a fire. It was a cold evening. A young girl came to the fire, too. She looked very closely at Peter and said, "Weren't you with that man called Jesus when He was arrested? Are you one of His friends?"

Peter had been so frightened when he had seen the soldiers tie up and drag Jesus away that he looked at the young girl and stammered, "I don't understand what you are saying." The thought of also being dragged away scared Peter.

"Surely you're His friend," said the young girl again. "No, no never," Peter cried. "I don't know who you are talking about!" The girl asked Peter three times, and three times Peter didn't tell the truth. Peter then heard a rooster crow just as Jesus had told him. Tears filled Peter's eyes. He was so sad that he, too, had let Jesus down just as Jesus said he would.

TALK TIME
What happened today with Peter, the disciple? Look at Day 338. Do you know someone who hasn't told the truth?

PRAYER TIME
Dear Lord Jesus, if ever anyone is hurt by lies, please would you comfort that person and make your goodness come out of sadness. Amen.

BIBLE TIME
Matthew 27: verses 11-26

Not true

The leaders of Jerusalem made up their minds about Jesus.
They hated everything that Jesus had done and taught the people.
They dragged Him off to their governor called Pilate. He was the top
man in Jerusalem, and he would see to it that Jesus suffered.

Pilate sat and glared at Jesus and said to the leaders, "What has
this man done wrong?" All the leaders shouted, "He leads people
the wrong way! He says that He is our King... but that isn't true."
Pilate looked at Jesus. "Do you hear what my leaders are saying
about you? Is it right what they say?" But Jesus stood still and said
nothing. The crowd shouted, "He will have to die!"

TALK TIME
*Has there ever been a time when someone has said untrue
things about you? What did you do or say?*

PRAYER TIME
*Dear Lord Jesus, I think you were very brave to stand up and
say nothing. Help me to deal with someone who doesn't tell the
truth in a way that makes you happy. Amen.*

BIBLE TIME
Matthew 27: verses 27-31

They made fun of him

The soldiers took hold of Jesus. They beat Him and hit Him hard. They put an old red robe on Him and jammed a make-believe crown made out of thorns onto His head. They made fun of Him and laughed at Him.

They knelt in front of Jesus, laughing and saying, "So you think that you're a king!"

The soldiers were enjoying all of this, but Jesus didn't say a word. His heart was heavy and sad.

The soldiers led Jesus away and made Him walk through the streets of Jerusalem carrying a big cross on His shoulders.

TALK TIME
What do you think when you read what happened to Jesus during this time?

PRAYER TIME
Dear Jesus, thank you that you went through all of this suffering for me and all my family, so that we may be forgiven and always be with you. Amen.

BIBLE TIME
Matthew 27: verses 32-33

A dreadful day

The crowds watched Jesus stumble and fall as He carried the cross through the streets of Jerusalem. Some of the people watching cheered, but others cried. One man was asked to come and help Jesus carry the cross... his name was Simon.

People pushed and jostled through the streets as they followed Jesus carrying the cross. Eventually, Jesus and the crowd came to a place called Golgotha just outside the city of Jerusalem.

Here they nailed Jesus to the cross by His hands and feet then pushed the cross into the ground. It was such a dreadful thing to do. Gradually, nearly everyone drifted away to leave Jesus to die. But His family and friends stayed and stood weeping in front of the cross.

TALK TIME
We still remember this important day today – it's called Good Friday. Can you talk about why Jesus died on the cross?

PRAYER TIME
Dear Jesus, although it must have been so very painful for you on this day, I want to thank you for dying for me so that you can forgive everything that I have done wrong. Amen.

BIBLE TIME
Matthew 27: verses 57-61

Jesus is buried

It was the evening, and a friend of Jesus' named Joseph took his body away to a special tomb.

Joseph gently and very tenderly wrapped the body of Jesus in a pure white cloth. He and some friends then rolled a big heavy stone in front of the entrance to the tomb.

Two friends called Mary and Mary Magdalene sat opposite the tomb weeping and crying. They couldn't believe that they had lost their best friend Jesus.

The next day Pilate, the governor, put a soldier in front of the tomb to stand guard.

TALK TIME
How do you feel about what happened to Jesus?

PRAYER TIME
Dear Jesus, thank you, for your love and that you died for me. Thank you for being my friend. Amen.

BIBLE TIME
Matthew 28: verses 5-6

An angel

Very early next day, at sunrise, three friends of Jesus went to visit His tomb. Their hearts were sad. They cried, and they held hands.

As they came toward the tomb, they saw that the stone had been rolled away, and they were fearful because they didn't know what had happened. They ran quickly toward the tomb. Jesus wasn't there!

Inside the tomb was an angel dressed in white.

"Don't be afraid," said the angel. "Jesus is not dead, He is ALIVE!"

TALK TIME
What a miracle! How would you have felt if you were one of the friends?

PRAYER TIME
Dear Jesus, I am so happy that you came alive! I want to tell all my friends how you came alive! Amen.

BIBLE TIME
Matthew 28: verses 8-10

Such joy

The angel in the tomb said to the two friends, "Don't be afraid. Go quickly to the other friends of Jesus and tell them what has happened."

What joy! They were so delighted to hear this good news. Their tears of sadness turned to tears of joy.

"Go," said the angel, "go and tell your friends to meet Jesus in Galilee. He will be waiting for you there."

They started to run... when suddenly in front of them appeared Jesus. Was it really Jesus? Both of the friends fell at His feet worshipping him. He really was ALIVE!

"Don't be afraid," Jesus said to them. "Go now and tell my friends that I will meet you all in Galilee."

TALK TIME
Do you know where Galilee is? Find it in an atlas.

PRAYER TIME
Dear Jesus, I love you because you are so gentle and loving. Help me to love others as you love us. Amen.

BIBLE TIME
Luke 24: verses 13-24

Friends chatting

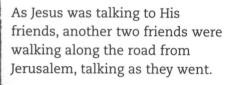

As Jesus was talking to His friends, another two friends were walking along the road from Jerusalem, talking as they went.

"Did you hear what happened today?" said one friend.

"Surely, they didn't let Jesus die?" said the other one sadly.

"Why did they allow such terrible things to happen to Jesus?" wondered the first friend.

Neither of them could work out why these horrible things had happened to Jesus.

"I know that Jesus could have done such wonderful things for our people," said the other friend.

"But friends say that He is now alive now... I really don't understand it at all!"

TALK TIME
Do you like asking questions? Whom do you like to ask when you have a question?

PRAYER TIME
Dear Jesus, you understand when we have questions. Please could you give me the right person when I have a question to ask. Thank you, dear Jesus. Amen.

BIBLE TIME
Luke 24: verses 15-30

Seeing Jesus

The two friends walked and talked together along the road outside Jerusalem. They couldn't understand why Jesus had died. As they talked, Jesus joined them... but they didn't know it was Jesus.

Jesus asked them, "What are you two talking about that makes you so sad?" One of the friends replied, "Haven't you heard what happened? Jesus died, but now He is alive! We don't understand it all." As they were nearing their village, the two friends asked Jesus for supper. They still didn't know who He was.

At suppertime, when Jesus served the bread and wine just as He had done a few days before at Passover, they suddenly saw that it was Jesus. He was ALIVE!

TALK TIME

Have you ever forgotten what someone looks like, even though you have met them before?

PRAYER TIME

Dear Jesus, I am so glad that I will always know you and will never forget your name. Amen.

BIBLE TIME
John 20: verses 24-29

Doubting Thomas

When all Jesus' friends met together, Thomas, one of the friends, said, "I'm not sure that I believe Jesus is alive." He continued, "Unless I see for myself the marks that He got when He died on the cross... I'm not sure that I believe it really is Jesus."

A few days later, the friends were gathered together in a room. They were still amazed at what had happened over the last few days... and now Jesus was alive!

Then Jesus came into the room. Jesus saw that Thomas was doubting, so He held out His hands and showed him the marks He got when He was held on the cross before He died.

As soon as Thomas saw the marks... he believed! "Dear Lord Jesus," said Thomas, "now I know it is you, and you are alive!"

Thomas didn't doubt anymore.

TALK TIME
Poor Thomas, it was hard for him to believe. Have you ever heard about something that you didn't believe until you saw it with your own eyes?

PRAYER TIME
Dear Lord Jesus, you know that we all doubt at some times but you lovingly answer those doubts for us when we come to you. Amen.

BIBLE TIME
John 21: verses 1-7

Such a lot of fish

A few of Jesus' friends had decided to go to Lake Galilee and push out their boat to do some fishing. The last few days had been full of surprises, with miracles happening such as Jesus dying and coming alive again! In Galilee it was peaceful, and on the lake they thought they would get some fish to eat. But all night they fished and caught nothing. Early in the morning a voice was heard from the shore, "Haven't you caught any fish?"

"No," they cried back, "we haven't." "Friends, throw your net over the other side of the boat," said the voice from the shore.

So they threw the heavy net across the other side of the boat and put it into the water. And guess what... a little while later they caught hundreds and hundreds and hundreds of fish!

TALK TIME
How would you like help from Jesus today?

PRAYER TIME
Dear Jesus, thank you for your kindness to the disciples.
Thank you, too, for your kindness to me and for always wanting to help me. Amen.

BIBLE TIME
John 21: verses 7-8

A big hug

When the friends had hauled all the fish into the boat, they wondered who the person was on the shore who told them to fish on the other side of the boat.

"Hey," said Peter, "I know who it is... it's Jesus!"

Peter was so excited that all he could think of was to go and greet Jesus on the shore!

So he jumped out of the boat with all his clothes on into the deep water and splashed his way toward the shore where Jesus stood.

Peter was dripping wet, but he was so pleased to see Jesus again that he gave him a big, big hug!

TALK TIME
If you were on that boat with the friends, what would you have done if you had seen Jesus?

PRAYER TIME
Dear Jesus, thank you that you always know what is best for us. Thank you that today I know you will provide all that I need... just for today. Amen.

BIBLE TIME
John 21: verses 15-19

Follow Jesus

"Come and join me for breakfast," Jesus said to His friends. "I have cooked some of the fish, and I have some bread." So they sat down with Jesus. They couldn't think of anything nicer than having a picnic with Him by the lake on a warm morning with the sun just coming up over the hills. When they had finished eating, Jesus turned to Peter and said, " Do you love me, Peter?"

"Yes, you know I do, Jesus," answered Peter.

"Then," said Jesus, "always follow me and take care of the people I will give to you. Soon I shall be leaving you and going to be with my Father in Heaven."

TALK TIME
Jesus wants us to take care of one another. How can you take care of people?

PRAYER TIME
Dear Jesus, I want to tell you that I love you and each day I want to take care of my family and friends. Amen.

BIBLE TIME
John 14: verses 1-4

A heavenly place

Just before Jesus went back to be with His Father, He talked to His friends about heaven. He said to them, "Don't let your hearts be troubled. Trust in God and me." And Jesus continued, "There are many rooms in Heaven for you all."

Jesus also told them what a big and wonderful place heaven is.

He then told them, "I am going to prepare a place for you in heaven, and then I will come back for you."

Jesus wanted everyone to know that everyone who believed in Him and His Father would join them both in heaven one day.

TALK TIME

Jesus said about heaven that He is preparing a room for you in His Father's house... that is, heaven. What do you think your room will be like?

PRAYER TIME

Dear Jesus, I'm so glad that I will see you in heaven. Thank you that you are preparing a place for us all, and thank you for making heaven so wonderful. Amen.

BIBLE TIME
Mark 16: verses 15-18;
Acts 1: verse 11

Jesus goes to heaven

They were talking together, and Jesus said to His friends, "When I have gone home to heaven... I want you to tell the world all about me and my Heavenly Father and what we have done for you."

He continued, "If you mention my name, there will be miracles and people will be healed. Don't be frightened. I will send the Holy Spirit to comfort you. He will guide you and give you power."

Then suddenly Jesus was carried up into the sky. The disciples just looked up with amazement.

Two men dressed in white stood beside them and said, "Why are you looking at the sky? Jesus has gone to heaven, but He will come back again."

TALK TIME
What story about Jesus would you like to tell a friend?

PRAYER TIME
Dear Jesus, thank you for promising the Holy Spirit who will guide us, teach us, and comfort us until we see you again. Amen.

BIBLE TIME
Acts 1: verses 12-14

In a room

The friends left the place where Jesus had suddenly gone up to heaven, and they started to walk back to Jerusalem. They talked and talked about everything that had happened and all that they had seen. It took them a long while to reach Jerusalem.

At last they reached Jerusalem, and they went to a place where they could stay. All of them were very weary as they entered the house and went upstairs to rest. A lot had taken place over the last few days... and now they were missing their special friend Jesus.

As they gathered in the room, they all decided to pray together.

TALK TIME

Do you pray with friends or family? What do you like to pray about with them?

PRAYER TIME

Dear Jesus, thank you for friends and family whom I can pray with. Thank you that you like us to gather together and speak to you. Amen.

BIBLE TIME
Acts 2: verses 1-4

Flames and wind

A while later, all the friends were gathered in an upper room together. There was suddenly a sound like the blowing of a very strong wind. It blew into the room where they were.

Little flames could be seen above each of the friends. Then something amazing happened... they were all filled with the Holy Spirit! Just as Jesus had said, they began to speak in other languages, praising God and filled with joy. Now they had the Holy Spirit inside them.

People heard about what had happened and were utterly astonished!

TALK TIME
Look at Day 356 to see what the Holy Spirit gives you.

PRAYER TIME
Dear Jesus, thank you that it was very clear to the friends of Jesus that the Holy Spirit came that day to guide us, comfort us, and give power to us. Amen.

BIBLE TIME
Acts 2: verses 8 and 11

Tell everyone

Wow, with the Holy Spirit in them, the friends were ready to tell everyone about Jesus and their Heavenly Father God.

At that time lots of people from many different countries lived in Jerusalem. When Jesus' friends were filled with the Holy Spirit, these people heard them speaking in their own language about Jesus... they were astonished!

The friends wanted to tell them everything about Jesus, what He had done, and also tell them about God their Heavenly Father.

They were even more excited!

TALK TIME

If you spoke to a friend about Jesus... what would you tell your friend?

PRAYER TIME

Dear Jesus, it is so amazing how the Holy Spirit came, and how people from different countries learned about you. I want to ask the Holy Spirit to teach me, too. Amen.

BIBLE TIME
Acts 2: verse 38

Be baptized

Peter went around Jerusalem telling everyone about how Jesus had died and how He had come alive again!

The friends of Jesus told everyone that Jesus would give them the Holy Spirit so that they could follow him.

"All you need to do is to say you're sorry to Jesus for going your own way," Peter told the people. "Then be baptized, and you will receive the Holy Spirit. The Lord is calling you to do this."

Many of the people heard what Peter was saying about Jesus and the Holy Spirit. Throughout that day hundreds and hundreds of people believed in Jesus. They were all baptized and received the Holy Spirit.

TALK TIME

Have you ever seen someone being baptized? Do you know why people get baptized? Look at Day 216 and see what John the Baptist said.

PRAYER TIME

Dear Lord Jesus, thank you for giving us your Holy Spirit. I don't want to go my own way... I want to do what you ask and I want to receive the Holy Spirit. Amen.

BIBLE TIME
Acts 1: verse 8

Power!

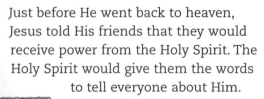

Just before He went back to heaven, Jesus told His friends that they would receive power from the Holy Spirit. The Holy Spirit would give them the words to tell everyone about Him.

Jesus said that His friends were to start in Jerusalem, then He told them to go to other parts of the country, telling as many people as possible about all that they had seen and heard about Him.

"Finally," Jesus said, "you are to go to all the world and tell everyone who I am and what I have done. Also tell them about my Heavenly Father."

That is the power of the Holy Spirit!

TALK TIME
Talking about Jesus is called witnessing. Have you ever been a witness?

PRAYER TIME
Dear God, thank you for giving us Jesus and your Holy Spirit. Help me to be a good witness wherever I go. Amen.

BIBLE TIME

Acts 9: *verses* 1-6;
Acts 13: *verse* 9

Jesus calls

After Jesus had gone to heaven, there was a man in Jerusalem called Saul. He hated the friends of Jesus and wanted them all put in prison because they were talking about Jesus so much!

Saul shouted terrible threats against them. One day, as he was traveling toward a place called Damascus, there was suddenly a brilliant light that shone around him. Saul fell to the ground. A voice spoke to him from Heaven. "Who are you?" asked Saul.

The voice from Heaven said, "I am Jesus. Now come and follow me."

Immediately Saul believed in Jesus, and his life was changed. His name became Paul, and from that day onward, he had many exciting adventures in different countries in the world telling many people about Jesus!

TALK TIME

Have you had an adventure recently? What happened?

PRAYER TIME

Dear Jesus, thank you that you ask me to talk about you. Help me to be bold when I talk about you. Amen.

371

BIBLE TIME
Acts 10: *verses 1-7 and 19-46*

Peter's vision

Peter, one of the disciples, was on a rooftop overlooking the sea when he had a vision from God. While Peter was wondering what the vision meant, some servants called for him. These servants were from a man named Cornelius, whose life was very different to Peter's.

"Why have you come?" asked Peter.

"Cornelius has sent us," the servants said. "He wants to hear what you have to say."

So Peter went with the servants to Cornelius's house, where he told them, "God has shown me that the good news of Jesus is for all people." As Peter talked about Jesus, Cornelius and all the crowd in his house believed in Jesus.

TALK TIME
There isn't anyone in the whole world that Jesus doesn't love. How does that make you feel?

PRAYER TIME
Dear Jesus, I thank you that everyone is special to you, and thank you that love me. Amen.

BIBLE TIME
Acts 16: verses 25-33;
Acts 27: verses 41-44

Further adventures

Paul had many adventures. One was when he went by boat to other countries, traveled across stormy, rough seas, and nearly got shipwrecked... but he knew that the Lord would look after him.

Paul wanted to tell as many people as possible about Jesus!

TALK TIME
Can you talk about the good news of Jesus? Can you remember what is so special about Jesus?

PRAYER TIME
Dear Lord Jesus, thank you that you are so special. Please help me to tell the good news about you to my friends. Amen.

BIBLE TIME
1 Thessalonians 4: verses 16-18

Coming back

One day Jesus has promised to come back to us. Won't that be wonderful! On that special day when Jesus returns... there will be first a trumpet blowing... and the voice of an angel will let us know just before it happens and then Jesus will come down from heaven. Jesus will come back as a king. Everyone will know that everything written in the Bible is true.

We don't know when that will be... but when He comes back to us we will be with Him forever and ever!

TALK TIME
What do you think about Jesus leaving heaven and coming back again?

PRAYER TIME
Dear Lord Jesus, I look forward to that special day when you return to us. Amen.

Dear young friends,

I pray you have enjoyed reading and looking at *Day by Day Bible* and that you have learned a lot about God your heavenly Father and his son Jesus.

After hearing all about Jesus and how much He loves you, you may like to ask Him into your heart.

Here is a prayer for you to say:

Dear Lord Jesus,
Thank you for loving me so much. Please forgive me for all the wrong things I have done. Please come into my heart and be my friend and help me to love you and obey you day by day.
Amen.

Now that you have prayed that prayer, have an enjoyable day with your new friend Jesus, knowing that He is with you.

With love from

Eira

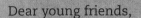